6

Agriculture Issues and Policies

Conservation Provisions in the 2014 Farm Bill and Associated Issues

AGRICULTURE ISSUES AND POLICIES

Additional books in this series can be found on Nova's website under the Series tab.

Additional e-books in this series can be found on Nova's website under the e-book tab.

AGRICULTURE ISSUES AND POLICIES

CONSERVATION PROVISIONS IN THE 2014 FARM BILL AND ASSOCIATED ISSUES

ARIANNA R. HILLS
EDITOR

New York

For permission to use material from this book please contact us:
Telephone 631-231-7269; Fax 631-231-8175
Web Site: http://www.novapublishers.com

Library of Congress Cataloging-in-Publication Data

ISBN: 978-1-61122-559-4

Published by Nova Science Publishers, Inc. † New York

CONTENTS

PREFACE

This book discusses the conservation provisions made in the 2014 farm bill, as well as associated issues.

Chapter 1 – The Agricultural Act of 2014 (2014 farm bill, P.L. 113-79) was enacted on February 7, 2014. After years of debate and deliberation, the enacted 2014 farm bill included a number of changes to the Conservation title (Title II), including program consolidation and reauthorization, amendments to conservation compliance, and a reduction in overall funding. Debate on the 2014 farm bill focused on a number of controversial issues. While many did not consider conservation to be controversial, nonetheless, a number of policy issues shaped the final version of the title and ultimately its role in the enacted farm bill.

Prior to the 2014 farm bill, there were over 20 distinct conservation programs. Discussion about simplifying or consolidating conservation programs to reduce overlap and duplication, and to generate savings, has continued for a number of years. The 2014 farm bill contained several program consolidation measures, including the repeal of 12 active and inactive programs, the creation of two new programs, and the merging of two programs into existing ones. Overall changes include the following.

- The act reauthorizes larger conservation programs through FY2018, including the Environmental Quality Incentives Program (EQIP), the Conservation Stewardship Program (CSP), and the Conservation Reserve Program (CRP).
- It authorizes a new Agricultural Conservation Easement Program (ACEP), which retains most of the program provisions in the repealed easement programs (Wetlands Reserve Program [WRP], easements

under the Grasslands Reserve Program [GRP], and Farmland Protection Program [FPP]). ACEP establishes two types of easements: agricultural land easements and wetland reserve easements.
- It authorizes a new Regional Conservation Partnership Program (RCPP) from the repealed partnership programs (Agricultural Water Enhancement Program [AWEP], Cooperative Conservation Partnership Initiative [CCPI], Chesapeake Bay Watershed Program [CBWP], and Great Lakes Basin Program for soil erosion and sediment control [GLBP]). RCPP creates partnership opportunities to target and leverage federal conservation funding for specific areas and resource concerns.
- It incorporates other programs, such as the Wildlife Habitat Incentives Program (WHIP) and grazing contracts under GRP, into larger reauthorized programs— EQIP and CRP, respectively.

One of the most controversial issues in the 2014 farm bill debate was whether federal crop insurance subsidies should be included on the list of program benefits that could be lost if a producer were found to be out of compliance with conservation requirements on highly erodible land and wetlands. Ultimately the 2014 farm bill did add federal crop insurance subsidies to the list of benefits that could be lost and extended limited protection for native sod in select states.

The 2014 farm bill also reduced funding for the Conservation title by \$3.97 billion over 10 years. Most farm bill conservation programs are authorized to receive mandatory funding, and the Conservation title makes up 6% of the total farm bill 10-year baseline, or \$58 billion of the total \$956 billion in mandatory funding authorized in the 2014 farm bill.

Agricultural conservation began in the 1930s with a focus on soil and water issues associated with production and environmental concerns on the farm. By the 1980s, agricultural conservation policies broadened to include environmental issues beyond soil and water, especially issues related to production (off the farm). Many of the current agricultural conservation programs were enacted as part of the 1985 farm bill (P.L. 99-198, Food Security Act of 1985). These programs have been reauthorized, modified, and expanded, and several new programs have been created, particularly in subsequent omnibus farm bills. While the number of programs has increased and new techniques to address resource problems continue to emerge, the basic approach has remained unchanged—voluntary farmer participation encouraged by financial and technical assistance, education, and basic and applied research.

The Conservation title (Title II) of the Agricultural Act of 2014 (P.L. 113-79), the 2014 farm bill, was largely uncontroversial. Both the House-passed farm bill (H.R. 2642) and the Senate-passed farm bill (S. 954) reauthorized many of the largest conservation programs and consolidated others to create new ones. The major difference between the two bills was the extension of conservation compliance provisions to the federally funded portion of crop insurance and the total reduction in funding for the title. Total mandatory spending for the title is projected at $28.3 billion over 5 years (FY2014-FY2018) and $57.6 billion over 10 years (FY2012-FY2023). The estimated spending impact of the 2014 farm bill's Conservation title is projected to decrease by $208 million over 5 years and close to $4.0 billion over 10 years.

Chapter 2 – The Conservation Reserve Program (CRP) provides payments to agricultural producers to take highly erodible and environmentally sensitive land out of production and install resource conserving practices for 10 or more years. CRP was first authorized in the Food SecurityAct of 1985 (P.L. 99-198, 1985 farm bill) and is administered by the U.S. Department ofAgriculture's (USDA) Farm Service Agency (FSA) with technical support from other USDA agencies. Participants offer land for enrollment through two types of sign-up: general and continuous. General sign-ups are competitive and only open during select times. Continuous sign-ups are not competitive, always open for enrollment, and offer additional financial incentives to those who qualify. Continuous sign-ups are targeted to specific environmental and resource concerns and operate through a number of initiatives. The largest and most well known is the Conservation Reserve Enhancement Program (CREP), which partners with states to address agricultural-related environmental concerns in specific geographic regions. While the majority of current acres enrolled were under general sign-ups (21.5 million acres), an increasing number are enrolled under continuous sign-ups (5.4 million acres).

Program and funding authority for CRP was extended in the American Taxpayer Relief Act (P.L. 112-240) and will now expire on September 30, 2013. Without reauthorization or an extension of authority the agency cannot approve any contracts or process any offers for enrollment. Congress continues to debate the reauthorization or extension of the 2008 farm bill, which authorized CRP to enroll up to 32 million acres. Bills considered, but not enacted, in the 112th Congress would reduce the authorized number of acres to 25 million and reauthorize the program through FY2017.

A number of factors have impacted CRP enrollment recently, mainly high commodity crop prices. These high crop prices have increased demand to put CRP acres back into production, even marginal acres. This pressure could potentially reduce the number of CRP acres offered for reenrollment once they have expired or cause existing current CRP participants to seek an early release from their CRP contract. Some participants also have cited a potentially low CRP rental rate compared to the market rental rate as a reason for decreased enrollment interest. Despite these factors, enrollment has increased under continuous sign-ups and demand for the program, in general, still exceeds the enrollment cap.

CRP has contributed to a number of environmental benefits including reduced soil erosion, improved water quality through wetlands and field buffers, reduced fertilizer use, and increased wildlife habitat. The recent expiration of a number of acres from the program, and a reduced reenrollment, has some concerned that a number of the environmental benefits gained under CRP could be lost or reduced if land is returned to production.

The Conservation Reserve Program (CRP) is the largest federal, private-land retirement program in the United States. The program provides financial compensation for landowners to voluntarily remove land from agricultural production for an extended period (typically 10 to 15 years) for the benefit of soil and water quality improvement and wildlife habitat.

The program was first authorized in the Food SecurityAct of 1985 (1985 farm bill, P.L. 99-198), initially as both a supply management tool for removing land from agricultural production, thus lowering commodity supply and potentially raising prices, and for providing environmental benefits. Currently over 27 million acres are enrolled in the program with total funding of close to $2 billion annually.

Acres enrolled in CRP have shown a number of positive environmental benefits including reduced soil erosion; water quality improvements through vegetative cover, buffer strips, and reduced fertilizer application; and wildlife population improvement from increased habitat. While a number of natural resource improvements are attributed to the program, the program contains a number of controversial elements as well, including the economic and environmental effect of haying and grazing on CRP acres; the expiration of program authority; and the early termination of contracts and reduced enrollment due to high crop prices. Program and funding authority for CRP expires September 30, 2013, and reauthorization or another possible extension is being debated by Congress as part of the larger farm bill reauthorization debate.

Chapter 3 – The Food Security Act of 1985 (P.L. 99-198, 1985 farm bill) included a number of significant conservation provisions designed to reduce production and conserve soil and water resources. Many of the provisions remain in effect today, including the two compliance provisions—highly erodible land conservation (sodbuster) and wetland conservation (swampbuster). The two provisions, collectively referred to as conservation compliance, require that in exchange for certain U.S. Department of Agriculture (USDA) program benefits, a producer agrees to maintain a minimum level of conservation on highly erodible land and not to convert wetlands to crop production.

Conservation compliance affects most USDA benefits administered by the Farm Service Agency (FSA) and the Natural Resources Conservation Service (NRCS). These benefits can include commodity support payments, disaster payments, farm loans, and conservation program payments, to name a few. If a producer is found to be in violation of conservation compliance, then a number of penalties could be enforced. These penalties range from temporary exemptions that allow the producer time to correct the violation, to a determination that the producer is ineligible for any USDA farm payment and must pay back current and prior years' benefits.

As Congress considers the reauthorization of farm policy in the next farm bill, issues related to conservation compliance have emerged. The reduction in soil erosion from highly erodible land conservation continues, but at a slower pace than following enactment of the 1985 farm bill. The leveling off of erosion reductions leaves broad policy questions related to conservation compliance, including whether an acceptable level of soil erosion on cropland has been achieved; whether additional reductions could be achieved, and if so, at what cost; and how federal farm policy should encourage additional reductions in erosion. These broad policy questions, in addition to general concerns of program oversight and implementation, continue to influence the farm bill debate.

One of the most controversial farm bill proposals involves adding crop insurance subsidies to the list of benefits that could be lost if a producer is found to be out of compliance. Federal crop insurance subsidies were originally included as a benefit that could be denied under the compliance provisions. However, they were removed in the 1996 farm bill to increase producer flexibility, while at the same time direct payments were added. Presently, high commodity prices have resulted in few or no counter-cyclical payments, leaving conservation program participation and direct payments as the remaining major benefits that might motivate producer compliance with conservation requirements. The Senate-passed farm bill (S. 954) would eliminate countercyclical and direct payments, and re-tie federal crop insurance subsidies to compliance requirements. The House-passed farm bill (H.R. 2642) would also eliminate direct payments, but does not tie crop insurance subsidies to compliance requirements. Re-tying crop insurance subsidies to compliance requirements has been met with mixed reviews. Most in the conservation and environmental community support the requirement, while some producer groups and the crop insurance industry are wary of the linkage. Separately, the Senate and House bills establish a "sodsaver" provision for new crop production on native sod. The provision reduces crop insurance premium subsidies and prohibits benefits under the Noninsured Crop Disaster or general commodity programs on land that has never been tilled. Conference negotiations to reconcile the two bills are ongoing.

Federal policies and programs traditionally have offered voluntary incentives to producers to plan and apply resource-conserving practices on private lands. It was not until the 1980s that Congress took an alternative approach to agricultural conservation through enactment of the Food Security Act of 1985 (P.L. 99-198, 1985 farm bill). The bill's more publicized provisions—the Conservation Reserve Program (CRP),[1] highly erodible land conservation (sodbuster), and wetland conservation (swampbuster)[2]—remain significant today. The latter two "conservation compliance" provisions require that in exchange for certain U.S. Department of Agriculture (USDA) program benefits, a producer agrees to maintain a minimum level of conservation on highly erodible land and not to convert wetlands to crop production. As Congress continues to debate the reauthorization of the farm bill, questions surrounding conservation compliance have arisen, such as how it works, whether it is effective, who it impacts, how it has changed over time, and how it might continue if current farm programs change. One of the most controversial issues has been whether conservation compliance should be tied to federal crop insurance subsidies.

In: Conservation Provisions …
Editor: Arianna R. Hills

ISBN: 978-1-61122-559-4

Chapter 1

CONSERVATION PROVISIONS IN THE 2014 FARM BILL (P.L. 113-79)*

Megan Stubbs

SUMMARY

The Agricultural Act of 2014 (2014 farm bill, P.L. 113-79) was enacted on February 7, 2014. After years of debate and deliberation, the enacted 2014 farm bill included a number of changes to the Conservation title (Title II), including program consolidation and reauthorization, amendments to conservation compliance, and a reduction in overall funding. Debate on the 2014 farm bill focused on a number of controversial issues. While many did not consider conservation to be controversial, nonetheless, a number of policy issues shaped the final version of the title and ultimately its role in the enacted farm bill.

Prior to the 2014 farm bill, there were over 20 distinct conservation programs. Discussion about simplifying or consolidating conservation programs to reduce overlap and duplication, and to generate savings, has continued for a number of years.

The 2014 farm bill contained several program consolidation measures, including the repeal of 12 active and inactive programs, the creation of two

* This is an edited, reformatted and augmented version of a Congressional Research Service publication R43504, prepared for Members and Committees of Congress dated April 24, 2014.

new programs, and the merging of two programs into existing ones. Overall changes include the following.

- The act reauthorizes larger conservation programs through FY2018, including the Environmental Quality Incentives Program (EQIP), the Conservation Stewardship Program (CSP), and the Conservation Reserve Program (CRP).
- It authorizes a new Agricultural Conservation Easement Program (ACEP), which retains most of the program provisions in the repealed easement programs (Wetlands Reserve Program [WRP], easements under the Grasslands Reserve Program [GRP], and Farmland Protection Program [FPP]). ACEP establishes two types of easements: agricultural land easements and wetland reserve easements.
- It authorizes a new Regional Conservation Partnership Program (RCPP) from the repealed partnership programs (Agricultural Water Enhancement Program [AWEP], Cooperative Conservation Partnership Initiative [CCPI], Chesapeake Bay Watershed Program [CBWP], and Great Lakes Basin Program for soil erosion and sediment control [GLBP]). RCPP creates partnership opportunities to target and leverage federal conservation funding for specific areas and resource concerns.
- It incorporates other programs, such as the Wildlife Habitat Incentives Program (WHIP) and grazing contracts under GRP, into larger reauthorized programs— EQIP and CRP, respectively.

One of the most controversial issues in the 2014 farm bill debate was whether federal crop insurance subsidies should be included on the list of program benefits that could be lost if a producer were found to be out of compliance with conservation requirements on highly erodible land and wetlands.

Ultimately the 2014 farm bill did add federal crop insurance subsidies to the list of benefits that could be lost and extended limited protection for native sod in select states.

The 2014 farm bill also reduced funding for the Conservation title by $3.97 billion over 10 years. Most farm bill conservation programs are authorized to receive mandatory funding, and the Conservation title makes up 6% of the total farm bill 10-year baseline, or $58 billion of the total $956 billion in mandatory funding authorized in the 2014 farm bill.

Agricultural conservation began in the 1930s with a focus on soil and water issues associated with production and environmental concerns on the farm. By the 1980s, agricultural conservation policies broadened to include environmental issues beyond soil and water, especially issues related to production (off the farm). Many of the current agricultural conservation programs were enacted as part of the 1985 farm bill (P.L. 99-198, Food Security Act of 1985). These programs have been reauthorized, modified, and expanded, and several new programs have been created, particularly in subsequent omnibus farm bills. While the number of programs has increased and new techniques to address resource problems continue to emerge, the basic approach has remained unchanged—voluntary farmer participation encouraged by financial and technical assistance, education, and basic and applied research.

The Conservation title (Title II) of the Agricultural Act of 2014 (P.L. 113-79), the 2014 farm bill, was largely uncontroversial. Both the House-passed farm bill (H.R. 2642) and the Senate-passed farm bill (S. 954) reauthorized many of the largest conservation programs and consolidated others to create new ones. The major difference between the two bills was the extension of conservation compliance provisions to the federally funded portion of crop insurance and the total reduction in funding for the title. Total mandatory spending for the title is projected at $28.3 billion over 5 years (FY2014-FY2018) and $57.6 billion over 10 years (FY2012-FY2023). The estimated spending impact of the 2014 farm bill's Conservation title is projected to decrease by $208 million over 5 years and close to $4.0 billion over 10 years.

POLICY ISSUES SHAPING THE CONSERVATION TITLE

Agricultural conservation has been a stand-alone title in farm bills beginning with the Agriculture and Food Act of 1981 (1981 farm bill, P.L. 97-98). Its significance has grown with each passing omnibus farm bill. Debate on the 2014 farm bill focused on a number of controversial issues. While many did not consider conservation to be controversial, nonetheless, a number of policy issues shaped the final version of the title and ultimately its role in the enacted farm bill.

Simplifying the Conservation Portfolio

Before the 1985 farm bill, few conservation programs existed and only two would be considered large by today's standards. Prior to the 2014 farm bill, there were over 20 distinct conservation programs with annual spending greater than $5 billion. The differences and number of these programs created general confusion about the purpose, participation, and policies of the programs (see below for a list of conservation program acronyms). Discussion about simplifying or consolidating conservation programs to reduce overlap and duplication, and to generate savings, has continued for a number of years. The 2014 farm bill contained several program consolidation measures, including the repeal of 12 active and inactive programs, the creation of two new programs, and the merging of two programs into existing ones.[1] Specific programmatic changes are discussed further in the "Program Changes" section.

Acronyms

ACEP	Agricultural Conservation Easement Program
AMA	Agricultural Management Assistance program
AWEP	Agricultural Water Enhancement Program (subprogram of EQIP)
CBWP	Chesapeake Bay Watershed Program
CCEP	Comprehensive Conservation Enhancement Program
CIG	Conservation Innovation Grants (subprogram of EQIP)
CREP	Conservation Reserve Enhancement Program (subprogram of CRP)
CRP	Conservation Reserve Program
CSP	Conservation Stewardship Program
CCPI	Cooperative Conservation Partnership Initiative
EFCRP	Emergency Forestry Conservation Reserve Program (subprogram of CRP
EPP	Environmental Easement Program
EQIP	Environmental Quality Incentives Program
FV	Farm Viability
FW	Farmable Wetlands program (subprogram of CRP)
FPP	Farmland Protection Program
GRP	Grassland Reserve Program

GLBP	Great Lakes Basin Program
HFRP	Healthy Forest Reserve Program
RCPP	Regional Conservation Partnership Program
Sodbuster	Highly Erodible Land Conservation
Sodsaver	Crop Production on Native Sod
Swampbuster	Wetland Conservation
VPAHIP	Voluntary Public Access and Habitat Incentive Program
WRP	Wetlands Reserve Program
WHIP	Wildlife Habitat Incentives Program

Compliance Requirements

Federal policies and programs traditionally have offered voluntary incentives to producers to plan and apply resource-conserving practices on private lands. It was not until the 1985 farm bill that Congress took an alternative approach to agricultural conservation with the enactment of highly erodible land conservation (sodbuster) and wetland conservation (swamp buster)—collectively known as "conservation compliance." Both provisions remain significant today and require that in exchange for certain U.S. Department of Agriculture (USDA) program benefits, including commodity support payments, disaster payments, farm loans, and conservation program payments, to name a few, a producer agrees to maintain a minimum level of conservation on highly erodible land and to not convert wetlands to crop production. One of the most controversial issues in the 2014 farm bill debate was whether federal crop insurance subsidies should be included on the list of program benefits that could be lost if a producer were found to be out of compliance. Ultimately the 2014 farm bill did add federal crop insurance subsidies to the list of benefits that could be lost and extended limited protection for native sod in select states (sodsaver). Specific programmatic changes are discussed further in the "Compliance Programs" section below.

Change in Program Type

Land retirement programs (e.g., the Conservation Reserve Program, CRP) provide producers with financial incentives to temporarily remove from production and restore environmentally sensitive land. In contrast, working lands programs (e.g., the Environmental Quality Incentives Program, EQIP) allow land to remain in production and provide producers with financial incentives to adopt resource-conserving practices. Over time, high commodity prices, changing land rental rates, and new conservation technologies have led to a shift in farm bill conservation policy away from the more traditional land retirement programs toward an increased focus on conservation working lands programs. Some of this shift has already occurred in the last decade and was continued in the 2014 farm bill as the percentage of mandatory program funding for land retirement programs has declined relative to working lands programs (see Figure 1).

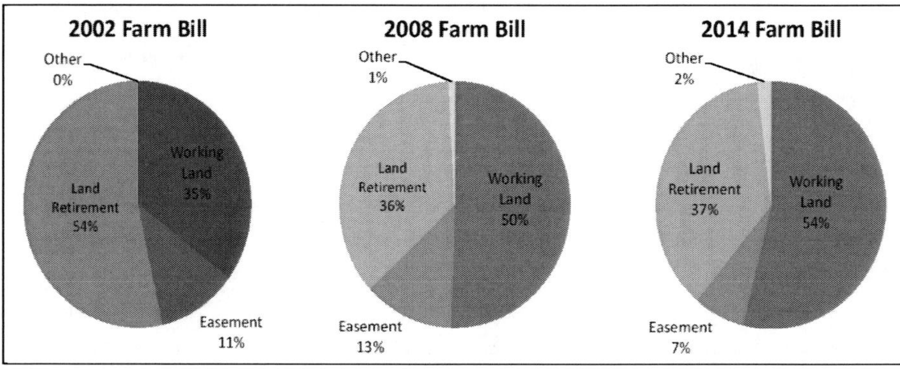

Source: CRS. Compiled from funding levels in annual appropriations, CBO baseline projections, and the CBO conference agreement score, http://www.cbo.gov/sites/default/files/cbofiles/attachments/hr2642LucasLtr.pdf.

Notes: Figures include mandatory funding for farm bill authorized conservation programs. The 2002 and 2008 farm bill charts cover the period after enactment to the next bill's passage and are adjusted for reductions, rescissions, and sequestration. The 2014 farm bill chart is based on the CBO estimate of direct spending for the life of the farm bill (FY2014-FY2018). Funding for conservation education, extension and research, and discretionary spending are not included.

Figure 1. Farm Bill Conservation Programs by Type.

Most conservation and wildlife organizations support both land retirement and working lands programs; however, the appropriate "mix" continues to be debated. Some are still divided between shorter-term land retirement programs such as CRP and longer-term easement programs such as the new wetland reserve easements under the Agricultural Conservation Easement Program (ACEP). Unlike land retirement programs, easement programs impose a permanent or longer-term land-use restriction that is voluntarily placed on the land in exchange for a government payment. Supporters of easement programs cite a more cost-effective investment in sustainable ecosystems for long-term wildlife benefits. Short-term land retirement program supporters cite the increased flexibility, which can generate broader participation than permanent or long-term easement programs.

There has also been a rising interest in programs that partner with state and local communities to target conservation funding to local areas of concern. These partnership programs leverage private funding with federal funding to multiply the level of assistance in a select area. A number of these partnership programs were repealed in the 2014 farm bill and replaced with the new Regional Conservation Partnership Program (RCPP). RCPP is designed to allow local organizations to partner with USDA to address resource concerns specific to that area. Partners are required to supply a significant portion of the overall cost of the project.

Budget and Baseline

Most farm bill conservation programs are authorized to receive mandatory funding. The Conservation title makes up 6% of the total projected farm bill spending, or $58 billion of the total $956 billion in 10-year mandatory funding authorized in the 2014 farm bill.[2] Like many titles in the farm bill debate, discussion was driven in part by the need for budget reduction. While a few titles did receive an increase in authorized mandatory funding over the projected baseline, three major titles did not, including Conservation.[3] Ultimately the Conservation title was reduced by $3.97 billion over 10 years, or 24% of the total $16.5 billion in savings (see **Figure 2**).[4] If the baseline to write the 2014 farm bill had not been reduced by sequestration, the enacted 2014 farm bill could have been credited for reducing conservation spending by about $6 billion over 10 years. But sequestration had already been factored into the baseline, so the official CBO score remains at $3.97 billion reduction from the Conservation title.[5]

In addition to sequestration, other budgetary dynamics may have an effect on farm bill conservation programs in the future. Since the 1996 farm bill, the number and size of conservation programs receiving mandatory funding has continued to grow. Currently the level of mandatory spending for conservation is roughly five times that of discretionary spending for conservation. For more than a decade, appropriators have placed limits on mandatory spending authorized in the farm bill, including a number of conservation programs. These limits are also known as CHIMPS, "changes in mandatory program spending." Many of these mandatory programs usually are not part of the appropriations process since funding is authorized in the farm bill for a specific time period (FY2014-FY2018) and is assumed to be available based on the statute and without further congressional action. Most of these conservation spending reductions, however, were at the request of both the Bush and Obama Administrations. The mix of programs and amount of reduction has varied from year to year. Some programs, such as CRP, have not been reduced by appropriators in recent years, while others, such as EQIP, have been repeatedly reduced below authorized levels. Even with these reductions, total mandatory funding for conservation programs has remained relatively constant at around $5 billion annually for the past five years. Conservation advocates are concerned that future CHIMPS would further deepen the cuts made by potential future sequestration and the 2014 farm bill reductions.

PROGRAM CHANGES

The 2014 farm bill reauthorized, repealed, consolidated, and amended a number of conservation programs. Generally, farm bill conservation programs can be grouped into the following categories based on similarities: working land programs, land retirement programs, easement programs, conservation compliance programs, and other programs and overarching provisions (see Table 1 and page 2 for a list of conservation program acronyms). Most of these programs are authorized to receive mandatory funding (i.e., they do not require an annual appropriation) and include authorities that expire with other farm bill programs at the end of FY2018. Other types of conservation programs—such as watershed programs, emergency programs, and technical assistance—are authorized in other non-farm bill legislation. Most of these programs have permanent authorities and receive appropriations annually through the discretionary appropriations process. These programs are not generally addressed in the context of a farm bill and are not covered in detail in this report, except for cases where the 2014 farm bill made amendments to the program.

General programmatic amendments, reauthorizations, and consolidations are discussed in the sections below. The **Appendix** provides a series of tables detailing the changes enacted in the 2014 farm bill as compared to prior law. The 2014 farm bill included several program consolidation measures, including the repeal of 12 active and inactive programs, the creation of two new programs, and the merging of two programs into existing ones. Table 1 and Figure 3 illustrate these consolidation measures.

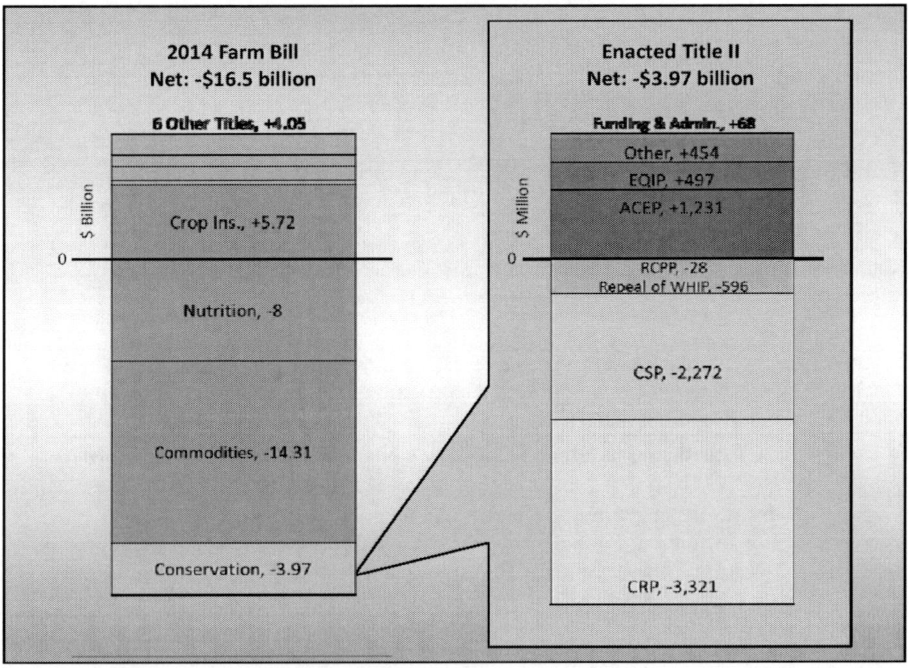

Source: CRS, using CBO cost estimates available at http://www.cbo.gov/publication/45049. For additional information, see CRS Report R42484, *Budget Issues That Shaped the 2014 Farm Bill.*

Notes: The CBO baseline is an estimate (projection) at a particular point in time of what future federal spending on mandatory programs would be under current law. The proposed changes to a current law are “scored” by CBO as either savings (negative, below the baseline) or spending (positive, above the baseline), as shown in this figure. The green shaded area provides more detail about the Conservation title and is not to scale. The Conservation title is stated in millions of dollars, whereas the remaining chart is stated in billions of dollars. A list of acronyms may be found on page 2.

Figure 2. Budget Scores of the 2014 Farm Bill (change in outlays relative to 10-year baseline FY2014-FY2023, by farm bill title).

Table 1. USDA Agricultural Conservation Programs by Category (after enactment of the 2014 farm bill, P.L. 113-79)

Farm Bill Agricultural Conservation Programs[a]
Working Lands Programs—allow private land to remain in production, while implementing various conservation practices to address natural resource concerns specific to the area.
• EQIP, CSP, AMA
Land Retirement Programs—provide federal payments to agricultural landowners for temporary changes in land use or management to achieve environmental benefits.
• CRP (CREP, FW)
Easement Programs—impose a permanent land-use restriction that is voluntarily placed on the land in exchange for a government payment.
• ACEP, HFRP
Compliance—prohibits a producer from receiving most federal farm program benefits (including conservation assistance) when conservation requirements for highly erodible lands and wetlands are not met.
• Highly erodible land conservation (sodbuster), wetland conservation (swampbuster), and sodsaver
Other Conservation Programs—programs that do not fit easily into the above categories. They are either regionally specific, use existing conservation program funds as leverage for partnership agreements with non-federal funding, or provide grants to states or research organizations.
• RCPP, CIG, VPAHIP
Non-Farm Bill Conservation Programs[b]
Technical Assistance Programs—provide landowners with science-based conservation information and technical expertise (e.g., engineering and biological) unique to the region and land use type. Usually do not include financial assistance.
• Conservation Operations (includes Conservation Technical Assistance, Survey, Soil Survey, Grazing Lands Conservation Initiative, and Plant Materials Centers)
Emergency Programs—provide disaster assistance for farmland rehabilitation and impairments to watersheds. Programs are usually funded through supplemental appropriation acts.
• Emergency Conservation Program (ECP) Emergency Watershed Protection (EWP) program (includes floodplain easements) and Emergency Forest Restoration Program (EFRP)
Watershed Programs—partner with local sponsors to carry out activities for soil conservation; flood prevention; conservation, development, utilization, and disposal of water; watershed surveys; and dam and flood structure rehabilitation.
• Watershed and Flood Prevention Operations (also referred to as the Small Watershed Programs, P.L. 566 and P.L. 534), and Watershed Rehabilitation program.

Source: CRS.

Notes: A list of acronyms may be found on page 2.

a. Generally, these programs originated or are reauthorized in farm bills. The 2014 farm bill repealed and consolidated a number of programs reflected in this table. Amendments to remaining programs are not reflected.

b. Generally, these programs originated outside of farm bill legislation and are considered to be in categories separate from most farm bill programs. Amendments to these programs may occur in farm bills, but those changes are not reflected in this table.

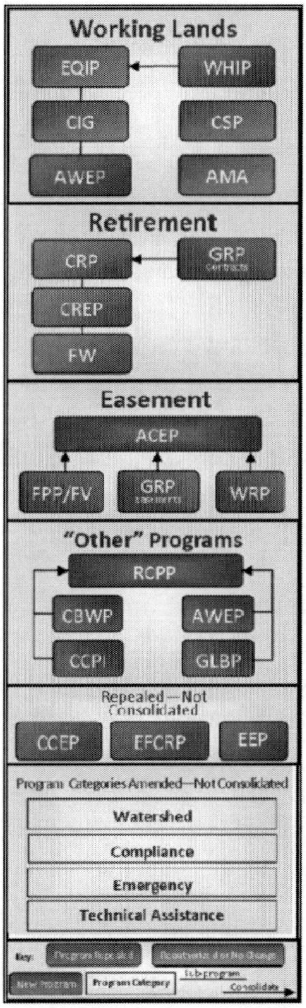

Source: CRS.

Notes: For a list of acronyms see page 2.

Figure 3. Conservation Program Consolidation in the 2014 Farm Bill.

Working Lands Conservation Programs

Working lands conservation programs are typically classified as programs that allow private land to remain in production, while implementing various conservation practices to address natural resource concerns specific to the area. Program participants receive some form of conservation technical assistance and planning to guide the decision on the most appropriate practices to apply, given the natural resource concerns and land condition. If selected, participants receive federal financial support to defray a portion of the cost to install or maintain the vegetative, structural, or management practices agreed to in the terms of the contract.

The two main working lands programs are the Environmental Quality Incentives Program (EQIP) and the Conservation Stewardship Program (CSP). Other working lands programs, such as the Wildlife Habitat Incentives Program (WHIP) and Agricultural Water Enhancement Program (AWEP), were repealed and incorporated into either new or existing programs. The Agricultural Management Assistance (AMA) program is generally amended in Title XI (Crop Insurance) because its original authorizing statute resides in the Federal Crop Insurance Act.[6] However, 50% of the funding is used as a conservation working lands program. Both the House- and Senate-passed farm bills included amendments to AMA, but none were adopted in the conference agreement.

Environmental Quality Incentives Program

The 2014 farm bill reauthorized and amended EQIP at a total of $8 billion between FY2014 and FY2018. The program provides financial and technical assistance to producers and landowners to plan and install structural, vegetative, and land management practices on eligible lands to alleviate natural resource problems. Eligible producers enter into contracts to receive payment for implementing conservation practices. Approved activities are carried out according to an EQIP plan developed in conjunction with the producer that identifies the appropriate conservation practice(s) to address resource concerns on the land. The program is reauthorized through FY2018 with a graduating level of mandatory funding—$1.35 billion (FY2014); $1.6 billion (FY2015); $1.65 billion (FY2016-FY2017); and $1.75 billion (FY2018). A similar progression was authorized in the 2008 farm bill; however, EQIP funding has been reduced in the annual appropriations process (CHIMPS) since 2003, and has never received its full authorized level of funding (see "Budget and Baseline" discussion above).

One of the major changes to EQIP in the 2014 farm bill was the incorporation of the WHIP. WHIP provided technical and financial assistance to private landowners to develop upland wildlife, wetland wildlife, threatened and endangered species, fish and other types of wildlife habitat. The program operated very similarly to EQIP, but had a direct focus on improving wildlife habitat. The 2014 farm bill repeals WHIP and amends EQIP to require that 5% of total EQIP payments benefit wildlife habitat. Other elements of WHIP are also incorporated, including the requirement for consulting with State Technical Committees annually to determine eligible wildlife habitat practices. The farm bill also reauthorizes the requirement that 60% of all EQIP payments benefit livestock. The two EQIP subprograms—AWEP and Conservation Innovation Grants (CIG)—are discussed further below. A detailed analysis of EQIP changes may be found in Table A-3.

Conservation Stewardship Program

The 2014 farm bill also reauthorized and amended CSP. The program provides financial and technical assistance to producers to maintain and improve existing conservation systems, and adopt additional conservation activities. Under CSP, participants must meet a "stewardship threshold" for a set number of priority resource concerns when they apply for the program, and then must agree to meet or exceed the stewardship threshold for additional priority resource concerns by the end of the five-year contract. In exchange, participants receive annual payments that are based, in part, on conservation performance. The program is limited by the number of acres available for enrollment each fiscal year, not total funding. Enrollment is offered through a continuous sign-up and applications are accepted year-round.

The 2014 farm bill amended CSP by making a whole-program substitution of statutory text. This did not mean, however, that all elements of the program changed as a result of the amendment. Primarily the changes reorganized the statutory language and refocused the program on generating additional conservation benefits. The amendments also raise the entry bar for participants, who are now required to address two priority resource concerns upon entry and meet or exceed one additional priority resource concern by the end of the contract. Contract renewal participants must meet the threshold for two *additional* priority resources concerns *or exceed* the threshold for two existing priority resource concerns. The 10% limitation on nonindustrial private forest land was lifted and flexible transition options are available for land coming out of CRP.

Another major change was the reduction in enroll able acres. Under the 2008 farm bill, CSP could enroll up to 12.769 million acres annually. The FY2014 farm bill reduces this to 10 million acres annually. This reduction creates an estimated $2.272 billion in savings over 10 years (see **Figure 2**). CSP was reduced in FY2011 and FY2012, when appropriators placed limits on mandatory spending (CHIMPS). The program was further reduced in FY2013 by sequestration. If these reductions continue, then the lower 10 million acre cap authorized in the farm bill would continue to slow program growth. At the end of FY2013, 59 million acres were enrolled in CSP.A detailed analysis of the programmatic changes may be found in Table A-2.

Land Retirement Programs

Land retirement programs provide federal payments to private agricultural landowners for *temporary* changes in land use or management to achieve environmental benefits. The primary land retirement program—the Conservation Reserve Program (CRP)—was reauthorized to enroll a decreasing number until FY2018. Other sub-programs of CRP, such as the Farmable Wetlands (FW) program, were also reauthorized and amended.

Conservation Reserve Program

CRP is the largest federal, private-land retirement program in the United States, spending more than $2 million annually. The program provides financial compensation for landowners (annual rental rate) to voluntarily remove land from agricultural production for an extended period (typically 10 to 15 years) for the benefit of soil and water quality improvement and wildlife habitat. The 2014 farm bill reauthorized CRP and reduced the enrollment cap from the previous 32 million acres to 24 million acres in FY2018. While CRP enrollment has fluctuated since its creation in the 1985 farm bill, recent enrollment has declined from its peak in FY2007 (with 36.8 million acres enrolled) to 25.6 million acres in FY2013. Further reduction in the farm bill was viewed as inevitable, given the fiscal challenges. Conservation and wildlife groups, however, remain concerned that reduced enrollment will impact critical species habitat and soil and water quality. Others point to the reduced enrollment as a product of high commodity prices, low rental rates, and declining interest in retiring land from production. The 2014 farm bill enrollment reduction created an estimated savings of $3.3 billion over 10 years.

The 2014 farm bill made several amendments to CRP, mostly centered on permitted activities. Emergency harvesting, grazing, and other use of forage are permitted, in some cases, without a reduction in rental rate, as well as livestock grazing for a beginning farmer or rancher. Other approved activities, such as annual or routine grazing, may continue to require a reduction in rental rate. The 2014 farm bill repealed the Grassland Reserve Program (GRP) and incorporated grassland contracts, similar to what was repealed under GRP, into CRP. The 2014 farm bill also allows CRP participants the opportunity to terminate their contract early if the land has been enrolled longer than five years and does not contain environmentally sensitive practices. A detailed analysis of the programmatic changes may be found in Table A-1.[7]

Easement Programs

Conservation easements impose a *permanent* land-use restriction that is voluntarily placed on the land in exchange for a government payment. The 2014 farm bill repealed the conservation easement programs—Wetlands Reserve Program (WRP), Farmland Protection Program (FPP), and GRP—and created a new Agricultural Conservation Easement Program (ACEP).

Agricultural Conservation Easement Program

The three repealed easement programs had similar but slightly different goals. All three programs were voluntary and sought to protect land from development by using permanent or long-term easements to achieve this goal. Participants were compensated based on a fair market easement value of the conservation easement. All three programs provided technical assistance and required some form of conservation planning and conservation practice adoption. The major distinctions among the three conservation easement programs were the type of land protected; whether production was allowed; the duration of the protection; and who held the easement. More information on these repealed programs is provided in the text box below.

The 2014 farm bill provides permanent baseline funding for ACEP. Funding became an issue when the 2008 farm bill was not reauthorized and easement programs such as WRP and GRP did not have baseline funding.[8] This meant that farm bill extensions did not restore funding for the programs, thus leaving them inactive until reauthorized.[9] While permanent funding was seen as a victory by many, others pointed out that total funding for the three repealed programs (WRP, GRP, and FPP) was higher in the previous five years than the total authorized level for ACEP for the next five years. Additionally, the enacted level of funding for ACEP was less than the levels in both the House- and Senate-passed farm bills.

Overview of Repealed Conservation Easement Programs

Wetlands Reserve Program (WRP)—WRP funded the purchase of easements (30 years or permanent), restoration agreements (usually 10 years in length), and 30-year contracts to assist land owners in protecting and restoring wetlands. It provided technical and financial assistance, and emphasized restoration to original natural wetland conditions where possible. The program was authorized to enroll up to 3.014 million acres at any one time nationwide.

Farmland Protection Program (FPP)—FPP provided funds to state, tribal, and local governments and nongovernmental organizations to help them purchase conservation easements from willing sellers to limit conversion of farmland to nonagricultural uses. USDA provided up to 50% of the fair market value of the conservation easement. The program was authorized to receive $200 million of mandatory funding in FY2014.

Grassland Reserve Program (GRP)—GRP used long-term rental agreements and easements to help landowners and producers restore and protect grasslands while maintaining them in a condition suitable for grazing using common management practices. Participants voluntarily limited future development and cropping uses of the land while retaining the right to conduct common grazing practices and operations related to the production of forage and seeding, subject to certain restrictions during nesting seasons of bird species in significant decline or protected under federal or state law. A grazing management plan was required for participants. GRP was authorized to enroll up to 1.22 million acres between FY2009 and FY2012.

ACEP retains most of the program provisions in the repealed easement programs by establishing two types of easements: agricultural land easements (similar to FPP and GRP) that limit non-agricultural uses on productive farm or grass lands, and wetland reserve easements (similar to WRP) that protect and restore wetlands. General program provisions are the same across both easement types, including ineligible land; subordination, exchange, modification, and termination procedures; and compliance requirements. Priority enrollment is given to expiring CRP acres.

Agricultural Land Easements

Similar to FPP, ACEP requires USDA to enter into partnership agreements with eligible entities to purchase agricultural land easements. Agreements with certified entities[10] are a minimum of five years with a review and recertification required every three years thereafter. Agreements with non-certified entities are three to five years in length. The entities agree to share the cost of the easement; purchase easements according to USDA's requirements; and enforce and monitor easements purchased. Also similar to the repealed FPP and GRP easements, agricultural land easements allow production to continue on the land while prohibiting nonagricultural uses.

ACEP provides funding to purchase easements through eligible entities and provides technical assistance for developing an agricultural land easement plan. The federal share of the easement may not exceed 50% of the fair market value[11] of the easement. The nonfederal share must be provided by the eligible entity and should be equivalent to the USDA share. Up to 50% of the nonfederal share may be a charitable donation or qualified conservation contribution from the private landowner, assuming the remaining nonfederal share is a cash contribution from the eligible entity. These cost-share requirements may be waived for grasslands of "special environmental significance." In this case, the federal share may be up to 75% of the fair market value of the easement and the nonfederal share cash requirement may be waived entirely. Agricultural land easements are permanent or for the maximum duration allowed under state law.

Wetland Reserve Easements

Much like WRP, wetland reserve easements are used to restore, protect, and enhance wetlands through the use of 30-year or permanent easements, or the use of 30-year contracts for Indian tribes. Landowners who have owned the land for at least 24 months prior to enrollment may submit an offer to USDA that will be evaluated based on its conservation benefits, cost effectiveness, and financial leverage. If selected, the landowner agrees to restore and maintain the wetland according to an approved wetland reserve easement plan. USDA, in return, provides technical and financial assistance for wetland restoration.[12] Landowners are compensated for the wetland reserve easement based on the fair market value of the land[13] and the length of the easement or contract.[14] USDA is also allowed to delegate the management, monitoring, and enforcement responsibilities of a wetland reserve easement to a separate authority.

A comparison of repealed program provisions (where applicable) to the new ACEP provisions may be found in Table A-4.

Other Conservation Programs

Regional Conservation Partnership Program

Similar to the consolidation of the easement programs, the 2014 farm bill consolidated a number of the "other" conservation programs that provided partnership opportunities or multi-state funding for watershed-scale projects. The Regional Conservation Partnership Program (RCPP) creates partnership opportunities to target and leverage federal conservation funding for specific areas and resource concerns. A number of eligible activities are defined in statute. However, consistent with the repealed programs, water quantity and water quality concerns continue to have a large presence in RCPP.

RCPP incorporates the Agricultural Water Enhancement Program (AWEP), the Cooperative Conservation Partnership Initiative (CCPI), the Chesapeake Bay Watershed Program (CBWP), and the Great Lakes Basin Program for soil erosion and sediment control (GLBP). Both AWEP and CCPI utilized partnership agreements to focus conservation program funds to targeted areas. The CBWP provided additional funds through existing conservation programs in the Chesapeake Bay watershed. The GLBP also targeted funding to a specific watershed, but unlike the other three programs, the GLBP did not receive mandatory funding and was last funded through appropriations in FY2010.[15]

RCPP uses 7% of available conservation program funds plus an additional $100 million annually in mandatory funding to address specific natural resource concerns in selected project areas. Project areas are defined by eligible partners and are selected through a competitive state or national competition. Partnership agreements (known as Regional Conservation Partnerships, RCPs) are for five years with a possible one-year extension. In addition to defining the project area, providing assistance, and possibly acting on behalf of the producers within the project area, partners must also provide a "significant portion" of the overall cost of the project. This leverages the partner's state, local, or private funding with RCPP's federal funding. Funds are also directed through "critical conservation areas" or CCAs. These areas are selected by USDA, are limited to eight nationwide, and expire after five years.[16] To be eligible for an RCPP contract, a producer must be located in either a CCA or RCP, but is not required to work with the sponsoring RCP partner and may choose to work directly with USDA. Figure 4 gives a general illustration of how RCPP funding may be obligated to producer contracts based on the 2014 farm bill.

RCPP contracts will follow the existing rules and requirements of the covered programs (i.e., EQIP, CSP, ACEP, and the Healthy Forest Reserve Program, HFRP). Alternative funding arrangements are allowed for multistate water resources agencies. Also, five-year payments may be made to producers participating in water quantity and quality projects, specifically, conversion from irrigated to dry land farming and improved nutrient management. A comparison of repealed program provisions (where applicable) to the new RCPP provisions may be found in Table A-5.

Conservation Innovation Grants

The Conservation Innovation Grants (CIG) program is a sub-program of EQIP. The program is intended to leverage federal investment, stimulate innovative approaches to conservation, and accelerate technology transfer in environmental protection, agricultural production, and forest management. The program was reauthorized in the 2014 farm bill through FY2018 at an unspecified funding level of total EQIP funding. The farm bill reauthorized and reduced the air quality component, which requires that payments be made through CIG to producers to implement practices to address air quality concerns from agricultural operations in order to meet federal, state, and local regulatory requirements. This air quality component was previously authorized at $37.5 million annually and is reduced to $25 million annually (between FY2014 and FY2018) in the 2014 farm bill. The farm bill also adds a reporting requirement that no later than December 31, 2014, and every two years thereafter, a report must be submitted to Congress regarding CIG funding, project results, and technology transfer efforts.

Compliance Programs

The 1985 farm bill included a number of conservation provisions designed to conserve soil and water resources. Two of the provisions remain in effect today—highly erodible land conservation (sodbuster) and wetland conservation (swamp buster). The provisions, collectively referred to as conservation compliance, require that in exchange for certain USDA program benefits, a producer agrees to maintain a minimum level of conservation on highly erodible land and to not convert wetlands to crop production.[17]

One of the most significant changes made by the 2014 farm bill was the addition of federal crop insurance premium subsidies to the list of benefits that could possibly be lost if a producer were found out of compliance. How compliance is calculated, where compliance provisions apply, and traditional exemptions and variances were not amended. The 2014 farm bill did create separate considerations when addressing compliance violations and the loss of federal crop insurance premium subsidies.

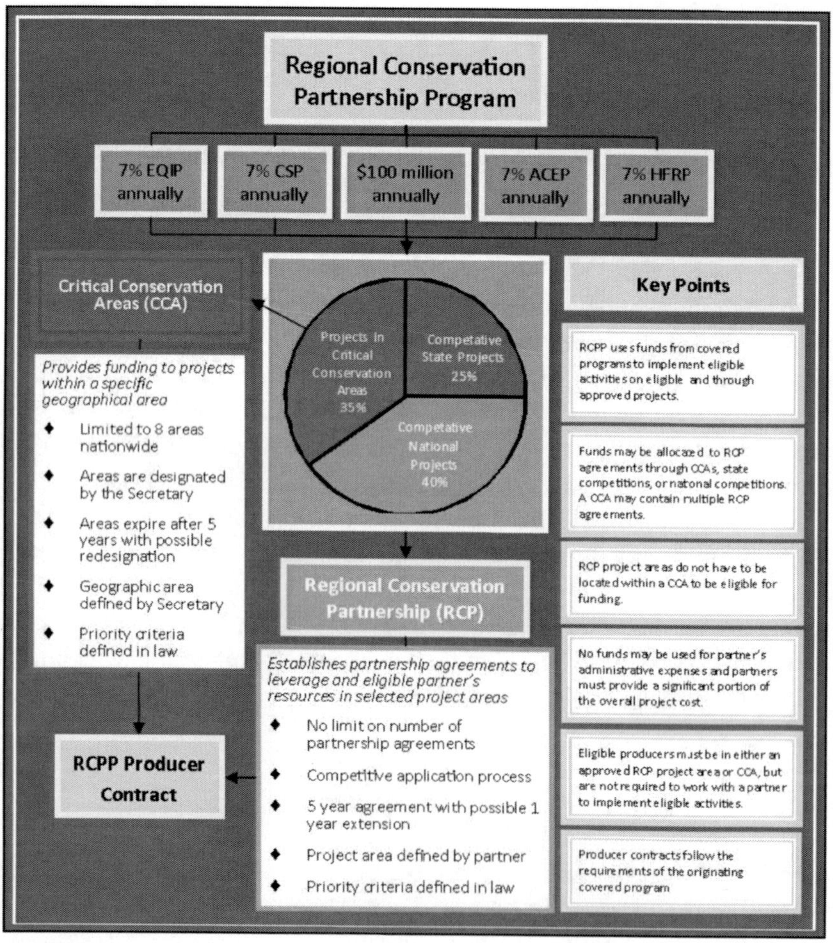

Source: CRS.

Figure 4. Regional Conservation Partnership Program (RCPP).

Highly Erodible Lands Conservation

The highly erodible land conservation provision (sodbuster) applies to land classified as highly erodible that was not in cultivation between 1980 and 1985 (i.e., newly broken land, referred to as sodbuster) and to any highly erodible land in production after 1990, regardless of when the land was put into production. Land meeting this classification can be considered eligible for USDA program benefits if the producer agrees to cultivate the land using an approved conservation plan. In addition to the application of an approved conservation plan, a number of exemptions are possible before benefits would be lost. These provisions were unchanged by the 2014 farm bill.

What did change under the 2014 farm bill was the list of USDA program benefits that could be lost if a producer were found out of compliance with the sodbuster provision. The list was expanded to "include any portion of the premium paid by the Federal Crop Insurance Corporation for a policy or plan of insurance under the Federal Crop Insurance Act."[18] This does not mean that producers cannot purchase a crop insurance plan through the federal crop insurance program; rather, if found out of compliance, they would be ineligible to receive the insurance premium subsidy paid by the federal government.[19] The loss of the insurance premium subsidy is not retroactive and would only take effect after all administrative appeals were exhausted.

The 2014 farm bill also extends the list of exemptions, allowing producers new to compliance requirements additional time (five reinsurance years)[20] to develop and comply with a conservation plan before the loss of federal crop insurance premium subsidies. Producers with compliance violations prior to the farm bill's enactment are allowed two reinsurance years to develop and comply with a conservation plan before the loss of the subsidies.

Wetlands Conservation

The "swamp buster" or wetland conservation provision extends the sodbuster concept to wetland areas. Producers who plant a program crop on a wetland converted after December 23, 1985, or who convert wetlands, making agricultural commodity production possible, after November 28, 1990, are ineligible for certain USDA program benefits. This means that, for a producer to be found out of compliance, crop production does not actually have to occur; production only needs to be made possible through activities such as draining, dredging, filling, or leveling the wetland. The wetlands compliance provision also includes a number of exempt lands.[21] These provisions were unchanged by the 2014 farm bill.

Table 2. Crop Insurance Eligibility and Wetland Conversions

Timing	Violation	Penalty
Newly Converted Wetlands— wetlands converted after February 7, 2014.	Converted wetland violation impacting five or more acres.	Ineligible for crop insurance premium subsidies, unless exemption applies.
	Converted wetland violation impacting less than five acres.	Ineligible for crop insurance premium subsidies, unless the landowner pays 150% of the cost of mitigation to a wetland restoration fund.
Prior Converted Wetlands—wetlands converted before February 7, 2014.	Any converted wetland violation.	Eligible for crop insurance premium subsidies. Ineligible for other USDA program benefits, unless exemption applies.
New Insurance Policies—wetlands converted after a new insurance policy or plan is made available for the first time.	Any converted wetland violation.	Ineligible for crop insurance premium subsidies, if prior conversions are not mitigated within two reinsurance years.

Source: 16 U.S.C. 3821(c)(2)

Notes: Table only applies to federal crop insurance premium subsidies. All other existing wetland compliance violations were unaffected by the 2014 farm bill provision.

Similar to sodbuster, the 2014 farm bill amends the wetlands conservation provision to include crop insurance premium subsidies as an ineligible benefit if found to be out of compliance. The amendment treats the time of wetland conversion differently (Table 2). The amendment also extends the list of exemptions for compliance violators, allowing additional time (one or two reinsurance years) for producers to remedy or mitigate the wetland conversion before losing crop insurance premium subsidies.

Producers must continue to self-certify their compliance with the sodbuster and swamp buster provisions. USDA is required to review certifications in a "timely manner"; otherwise, producers will be held harmless with regard to eligibility even if a subsequent violation is found. Producers who do not self-certify and are found to be in violation must pay an "equitable contribution" to a wetland restoration fund, not to exceed the premium subsidy amount. USDA retains sole responsibility for implementing the conservation compliance provisions.

The 2014 farm bill also amended the wetland mitigation banking program. Under wetlands conservation, compliance violators have the option of mitigating the violation through the restoration of a converted wetland, the enhancement of an existing wetland, or the creation of a new wetland.[22] Debate over these wetland mitigation requirements arose during the 2014 farm bill and centered on the concern that some producers were required to mitigate wetlands with a greater than 1-to-1 acreage ratio. This is allowed by statute if "more acreage is needed to provide equivalent functions and values that will be lost as a result of the wetland conversion to be mitigated."[23] The House-passed farm bill would have limited wetland mitigation to not more than a 1-to-1 acreage ratio. The Senate-passed farm bill would have required a study to assess the use of wetland mitigation, determine impacts on wildlife habitat, and provide recommendations for improving wetland mitigation procedures. Ultimately, the conference agreement adopted neither the House nor Senate provision and instead provided $10 million in mandatory funding for mitigation banking efforts. While the provision remains unchanged in statute, the conference report (H.Rept. 113-333) includes language encouraging USDA to use a wetland mitigation ratio not to exceed 1-to-1 acreage.

Sodsaver

The 2008 farm bill created a compliance provision under the Crop Insurance title, known as sodsaver. The sodsaver provision would have made producers who planted crops (five or more acres) on native sod ineligible for crop insurance and the noninsured crop disaster assistance (NAP) program[24] for the first five years of planting. The 2008 farm bill limited the provision to virgin prairie converted to cropland in the Prairie Pothole National Priority Area, but only if elected by the state. Ultimately no governors opted to participate in the program and sodsaver was never activated.

The Crop Insurance title (Title XI) of the 2014 farm bill amended and expanded the sodsaver provision.[25] Unlike the 2008 sodsaver provision, there is no opt-in requirement and the provision became effective upon enactment. The sodsaver provision also applies to native sod in six states—Minnesota, Iowa, North Dakota, South Dakota, Montana, and Nebraska—rather than only the area covered by the Prairie Pothole National Priority Area. Crop insurance premium subsidies will now be reduced by 50 percentage points for production on native sod during the first four years of planting.[26] Crops planted on native sod will have reduced benefits under NAP. The farm bill also clarified that native sod may include land that has never been tilled or cases where the producer cannot substantiate that the ground has ever been tilled.

Crop yield guarantees might also be affected for crop insurance policies. The yield guarantee for a crop insurance policy is a producer's "normal" crop yield based on actual production history (APH). In the absence of actual yield data (e.g., production on native sod or no yield documentation on existing fields), a "transition yield" (T-yield) is assigned, which is based on a portion of 10-year average county yields for the crop. The 2014 farm bill sets the T-yield factor on native sod equal to 65% of the 10-year average county yield for production on native sod. For other cropland, the percentage can be higher depending on the number of years of actual data included in the APH. Also, "yield substitution" is not allowed; that is, low farm yields must be used in the APH rather than replacing them with potentially higher T-yields as allowed for other cropland. This is expected to reduce the incentive to produce on native sod.

APPENDIX. COMPARISON OF CONSERVATION PROVISIONS ENACTED IN THE 2014 FARM BILL TO PRIOR LAW

This appendix includes a series of tables arranged by subtitle included in Title II of the Agricultural Act of 2014 (P.L. 113-79). U.S. Code citations are included in brackets in the "Prior Law" column. Corresponding section numbers in P.L. 113-79 are included in brackets in the "Enacted 2014 Farm Bill" column. Funding for most Title II programs is covered in the "Funding and Administration" subtitle (Table A-7). Where appropriate, funding levels are repeated within a program's corresponding subtitle table.

Table A-1. Subtitle A—Conservation Reserve Program

Prior Law	Enacted 2014 Farm Bill (P.L. 113-79)
General Provisions	
Sec.1231(a-b) of the Food Security Act of 1985 (FSA) (P.L. 99-198, or the 1985 farm bill), as amended, authorizes the CRP through FY2013. CRP provides annual rental payments to producers to replace crops highly erodible and environmentally sensitive land with long-term resource conserving plantings. **[16 U.S.C. 3831(a-b)]**	Extends authorization through FY2018. Adds grasslands to list of eligible lands, which is consistent with the consolidation of Grassland Reserve Program (GRP) rental agreements under CRP (also see Duties of the Secretary, sec. 1233 of FSA). Amends eligible land definition for land not enrolled in CRP to include filterstrips and land enrolled in other conservation practices. **[Sec. 2001(a-b)]**
Sec. 1231(c) of the FSA, as amended, determines the planting status of certain land. **[16 U.S.C. 3831(c)]**	Deletes language allowing land enrolled in the Water Bank Program and cropland expiring in CY2000-CY2002 to be enrolled. **[Sec. 2001(c)]**
Sec. 1231(d) of the FSA, as amended, authorizes the maximum acreage enrollment levels; the program is currently authorized through FY2013 to enroll up to 32 million acres. **[16 U.S.C. 3831(d)]**	Reduces enrollment to 27.5 million acres in FY2014; 26 million acres in FY2015; 25 million acres in FY2016; and 24 million acres in both FY2017 and FY2018. Also caps grassland enrollment at 2 million acres between FY2014- FY2018. Gives expiring CRP acres priority enrollment for grassland contracts. Grassland sign-up is continuous with one or more ranking periods. **[Sec. 2001(d)]**
Sec. 1231(e) of the FSA, as amended, defines the duration of contracts. **[16 U.S.C. 3831(e)]**	Amends language for land devoted to hardwood trees, shelterbelts, windbreaks, or wildlife corridors to allow flexible contract lengths beyond the current 10-15 years. **[Sec. 2001(e)]**
Sec. 1231(f) of the FSA, as amended, lists conservation priority areas as the Chesapeake Bay Region, the Great Lakes Region, and Long Island Sound. Watersheds with significant	Deletes the watershed-specific language, but retains the use of conservation priority areas as determined by USDA. **[Sec. 2001(f)]**

Table A-1. (Continued)

Prior Law	Enacted 2014 Farm Bill (P.L. 113-79)
adverse water quality or habitat impacts related to agricultural production activities are eligible for priority designation. Areas expire after five years or upon application of the state. **[16 U.S.C. 3831f]**	
Farmable Wetlands Program	
Sec. 1231B(a-f) of the FSA, as amended, authorizes a pilot program for up to one million acres of wetland and buffer acreage in CRP. **[16 U.S.C. 3831b]**	Renames the pilot program "Farmable Wetlands Program." Reauthorizes the program through FY2018, and clarifies language related to constructed wetlands receiving water from agricultural drainage. Reduces acreage limitation from one million acres to 750,000 acres. **[Sec. 2002]**
Duties of Owners and Operators	
Sec. 1232(a)(8) of the FSA, as amended, establishes approved use of harvesting, grazing, and wind turbine use on CRP acres. **[16 U.S.C. 3832(a)(8)]**	Deletes language related to harvesting, grazing, and wind turbine use on CRP acres and adds similar language under the Duties of the Secretary section (sec. 1233 of FSA). **[Sec. 2003(a)]**
Sec. 1232(b & d) of the FSA, as amended, requires a conservation plan on all CRP acres and reduces rental payment for certain authorized uses. **[16 U.S.C. 3832(b & d)]**	Amends conservation plan language by removing possible base acre retirement. Deletes rental payment reduction requirement for certain authorized activities and adds similar language under the Duties of the Secretary section (sec. 1233 of FSA). **[Sec. 2003(b-c)]**
Duties of the Secretary	
Sec. 1233 of the FSA, as amended, specifies the duty of USDA to make cost-share payments and rental payments. **[16 U.S.C. 3833]**	Deletes the current section and adds new section. In return for a CRP contract, USDA makes cost-share and rental payments. Certain permitted activities are allowed if consistent with an approved conservation plan and are subject to restrictions for nesting birds that are economically significant, in decline, or conserved by law.

Prior Law	Enacted 2014 Farm Bill (P.L. 113-79)
	Emergency harvesting, grazing, and other use of forage are permitted without a reduction in rental rate. Livestock grazing for a beginning farmer or rancher is permitted without a reduction in rental rate. Other certain permitted activities (harvesting, grazing, and wind turbines) are permitted in exchange for not less than a 25% reduction in rental rates. Grazing, harvesting, and fire suppression are permitted on enrolled grasslands. In exchange for a reduced rental rate, a landowner may install land improvement practices up to one year before the CRP acres expire. This land may not reenroll in CRP for five years. **[Sec. 2004]**
Payments	
Sec. 1234 of the FSA, as amended, establishes a framework for calculating annual rental payments. **[16 U.S.C. 3834]**	Specifies that tree and shrub maintenance cost share payments are limited to between two and four years beginning on the date of planting. Adds the requirement that incentive payments be limited to no more than 150% of the cost of thinning or other practices conducted. Amends rental payment calculation to include grassland contracts for not more than 75% of the grazing value. Adds the requirement that the National Agricultural Statistics Service (NASS) conduct a rental rate survey no less than once a year. Dryland cash rental rates may also be used as a factor for determining annual rental rates. Deletes language allowing for in-kind commodities as a form of CRP payment. Payments must be made in cash and may be in advance of performance determinations. **[Sec. 2005]** Limits of $10 million for

Table A-1. (Continued)

Prior Law	Enacted 2014 Farm Bill (P.L. 113-79)
	thinning activities between FY2014-FY2018 **[Sec. 2601(a)]**.
Contract Requirements	
Sec. 1235(e) of the FSA, as amended, allows owners and operators to terminate a contract entered into before January 1, 1995, at any time if the contract has been effect for at least five years. Land with filterstrips, waterways, strips adjacent to riparian areas, windbreaks, shelterbelts, erodibility index of more than 15, and other land of high environmental value (e.g., wetlands) are not eligible for early release. The contract termination becomes effective 60 days after the participants notice. Rental payments are prorated and conservation compliance requirements remain in effect. **[16 U.S.C. 3835(e)]**	Allows owners and operators to terminate their CRP contracts in FY2015 if the contract has been in place for at least five years. Adds to the list of excepted land, including land with: hardwood trees, wildlife habitat, duck nesting habitat, pollinator habitat, upland bird habitat buffer, wildlife food plots, State Acres for Wildlife Enhancement (SAFE), shallow water areas for wildlife, rare and declining habitat, farmable wetlands, restored wetlands, diversions, erosion control structures, flood control structures, contour grass strips, living snow fences, salinity reducing vegetation, cross wind trap strips, sediment retention structures, federally designated wellhead protection areas, an easement under CRP, and average width of a perennial stream or permanent water body, and a CREP contract. Terminations become effective upon approval. **[Sec. 2006(a)]**
Sec. 1235(f) of the FSA, as amended, facilitates the transfer of CRP acres from a retiring owner to a beginning/socially-disadvantaged producer to return land to production, and allows new owner to begin land improvements or start organic certification process one year before CRP contract expires. **[16 U.S.C. 3835(f)]**	Adds "veteran farmer or rancher" as eligible individuals for the transition option, in addition to beginning farmer or rancher. Specifies that approved land improvements include preparing to plant an agricultural crop. **[Sec. 2006(b)]** Reauthorizes and increases the limit on the CRP transition option to $33 million total between FY2014-FY2018. **[Sec. 2601(a)]**
No comparable provision	Allows landowners to enroll in CSP (see Table A-2) and conduct activities required under CSP in the final year of

Prior Law	Enacted 2014 Farm Bill (P.L. 113-79)
	the CRP contract without violating the terms of the contract. Allows USDA to terminate or modify a CRP contract if eligible land is transferred into ACEP (see Table A-4). **[Sec. 2006(c)]**
Sec. 1235A of the FSA, as amended, allows land enrolled in CRP before enactment of the 1990 farm bill (P.L. 101- 624, November 28, 1990) to convert vegetative cover to hardwood trees or restored wetlands **[16 U.S.C. 3835a]**	Repeals provision. **[Sec. 2007]**
No comparable provision.	Provides transition language stating that changes made by the 2014 farm bill do not affect the validity or terms of existing contracts. Allows CRP participants to update their current contract to reflect the new terms and conditions under Sec. 2004 (permitted activities). **[Sec. 2008]**
Funding	
Sec. 1241(a)(1) of the FSA, as amended, allows the use of funds, facilities, and authorities of the Commodity Credit Corporation to carry out CRP. Limits payments for thinning activities to $100 million total between FY2009- FY2013 and payments for the transition assistance to $25 million total for FY2009-2013. **[16 U.S.C. 3841(a)(1)]**	Reduces limit for incentive activities (see **Sec. 2005**) to $10 million total between FY2014-FY2018 and increases limit for transition assistance (see **Sec. 2006**) to $33 million total between FY2014-FY2018. **[Sec. 2601(a)]**

Source: CRS.

Table A-2. Subtitle B—Conservation Stewardship Program

Prior Law	Enacted 2014 Farm Bill (P.L. 113-79)
Definitions	
Sec. 1238D of the Food Security Act of 1985 (FSA), as amended, defines program terms for CSP, including: conservation activities,	Deletes the definition of 'conservation measurement tool.' Moves the definition of 'agricultural operation' and 'eligible land' from the Conservation Stewardship

Table A-2. (Continued)

Prior Law	Enacted 2014 Farm Bill (P.L. 113-79)
conservation measurement tools, conservation stewardship plan, priority resource concern, program, resource concern, and stewardship threshold. **[16 U.S.C. 3838d]**	Program section (sec. 1238E of FSA) to the list of definitions. Amends the definition of 'eligible land' to specify nonindustrial private forestland rather than agroforestry, removes the term prairie land, and states pastureland rather than improved pastureland. Merges the term 'resource concern' with the definition of 'priority resource concern.' **[Sec. 2101(a)]**
Conservation Stewardship Program	
Sec. 1238E of the FSA, as amended, establishes the CSP program for FY2009-FY2014. Eligible land includes private agricultural land, tribal agricultural land (that has been planted to crops in four of preceding six years), and nonindustrial private forest land. Land enrolled in CRP or WRP is considered ineligible. **[16 U.S.C. 3838e]**	Reauthorizes the program through FY2018. Moves definition of 'eligible land' to the definition section (sec. 1238D of FSA, discussed above) and removes nonindustrial private forest land limit of not more than 10% of total annual acres. Permits CSP enrollment of land under a CRP contract provided the CRP contract is scheduled to expire at the end of the year in which the land is enrolled in CSP; and CRP payments for the land cease prior to the date of the first CSP payment. Land enrolled in a wetland reserve easement through ACEP is ineligible. Retains the ineligibility for land not planted in crops for four of the preceding six years. **[Sec. 2101(a)]**
Stewardship Contracts	
Sec. 1238F of the FSA, as amended, establishes contract requirements for addressing at least one resource concern upon application and meeting or exceeding the threshold for at least one priority resource concern by the end of the contract. Establishes ranking criteria of applications, contract	Increases the entry requirement to address two resource concerns upon applying and meeting or exceeding the threshold for at least one additional priority resource concern. Adds expiring CRP acres transitioning to production as a consideration for ranking applications. Adds that USDA must agree to the transfer of duties and rights when there is a change of interest in the land under CSP

Prior Law	Enacted 2014 Farm Bill (P.L. 113-79)
provisions, contract renewal, and contract terminations. **[16 U.S.C. 3838f]**	contract. Requires contract renewal participants to meet the threshold for two *additional* priority resources concerns OR exceed the threshold for two *existing* priority resource concerns. Moves the 'coordination with organic certification' provision to the Duties of the Secretary section (sec. 1238G of FSA). Removes the 'On Farm Research and Demonstration or Pilot Testing' provision. **[Sec. 2101(a)]**
Duties of the Secretary	
Sec, 1238G of the FSA, as amended, outlines the duties of USDA, including offering continuous enrollment with at least one ranking period per year, identifying between three to five priority resource concerns, and developing a conservation measurement tool. Limits acreage enrollment to 12,769,000 acres for each fiscal year 2008 through 2017. Requires a national average rate of $18 per acre (to include all costs). Payments may be based on the costs incurred, income foregone, and expected environmental benefits. In general, payments are made at the beginning of each fiscal year and are limited to a total of $200,000 for all CSP contracts during any five-year period. **[16 U.S.C. 3838g]**	Increases the number of priority resource concerns identified by USDA to not less than five. Removes references to a conservation measurement tool. Reduces the number of enrollable acres to 10 million acres for each fiscal year 2014 through 2022. Adjusts the payment limit aggregate to $200,000 for all CSP contracts between FY2014 and FY2018. In addition to costs incurred, income foregone, and expected environmental benefits, annual payments are also based on the extent concerns are addressed through conservation activities, level of stewardship maintained over time, and degree which activities are integrated across the entire operation. Requires a prorated performance over the life of the contract to create equal payments each fiscal year. Removes data collection requirements. **[Sec. 2101(a)]**
No comparable provision.	Provides transition language stating that changes made by the 2014 farm bill do not affect the validity or terms of existing contracts. Funding for existing CSP contracts may be made from current year funds. **[Sec. 2101(b)]**

Source: CRS.

Table A-3. Subtitle C—Environmental Quality Incentives Program

Prior Law	Enacted 2014 Farm Bill (P.L. 113-79)
Purpose	
Sec. 1240 of the Food Security Act of 1985 (FSA), as amended, authorizes EQIP, stating its purpose as promoting production and environmental quality as compatible goals, and optimizing environmental benefits by assisting producers: (1) to comply with national regulatory requirements; (2) to avoid the need for regulation; (3) to install and maintain conservation practices; (4) to make cost-effective changes to current production systems, and (5) to reduce administrative burdens by consolidating planning and regulatory compliance. **[16 U.S.C. 3839aa]**	Removes the purpose of requiring the reduction of administrative burdens on the producer through consolidating conservation planning and streamlining regulatory compliance processes. Adds wildlife habitat improvement and development practices to the purpose list. **[Sec. 2201]**
Definitions	
Sec. 1240A of the FSA, as amended, defines six terms: eligible land, National Organic Program, organic system plan, payment, practice, and program. **[16 U.S.C. 3839aa-1]**	Incorporates the definition of the National Organic Program into the definition of an organic system plan. **[Sec. 2202]**
Establishment and Administration	
Sec. 1240B(a-b) of the FSA, as amended, authorizes EQIP through FY2015. Contracts are one to ten years in length. **[16 U.S.C. 3839aa-2(a-b)]**	Reauthorizes EQIP through FY2018. Removes the minimum one-year contract length requirement. **[Sec. 2203(1-2)]**
Sec. 1240B(d) of the FSA, as amended, limits EQIP payments to not more than 75% of the cost (up to 90% for limited resource, socially disadvantaged farm or rancher, or a beginning farmer or rancher) and not more than 100% of income forgone. Greater significance is provided for determining income foregone	Broadens the list of practices afforded greater significance when determining income foregone. Adds veteran farmer or rancher to the list of certain producers eligible for cost-share rates up to 90% and advanced payments. Increases the limit for advanced payments to certain producers to 50% and requires advanced payments not

Prior Law	Enacted 2014 Farm Bill (P.L. 113-79)
payments for specific management practices. Advance payments for certain producers are limited to 30% of the cost-share rate. **[16 U.S.C. 3839aa-2(d)]**	used within 90 days to be returned. **[Sec. 2203(3)]**
Sec. 1240B(f) of the FSA, as amended, requires that 60% of EQIP payments go to practices related to livestock production requirement between FY2008-FY2013. **[16 U.S.C. 3839aa-2(f)]**	Extends through FY2018 the requirement that 60% of payments be for livestock production. Requires a minimum of 5% of annual funds go to payments benefiting wildlife habitat through FY2018 (see Sec. 2203(5)). **[Sec. 2203(4)]**
Sec. 1240N of the FSA, as amended, authorizes the Wildlife Habitat Incentives Program (WHIP), providing cost-sharing to landowners who improve habitat. Authorized to receive mandatory funding of $85 million annually through FY2013. **[16 U.S.C. 3839bb-1]**	Adds a new provision under EQIP specifically for wildlife habitat incentive practices. Language is similar to the WHIP, which is repealed in Sec. 2707. Requires USDA to consult with State Technical Committees once a year when determining eligible practices. **[Sec. 2203(5)]**
Evaluation of Applications	
Sec. 1240C(b) of the FSA, as amended, identifies priorities to program applications. Gives higher priority for producers using cost-effective conservation practices to achieve environmental benefits. **[16 U.S.C. 3839aa- 3(b)]**	Changes "environmental benefits" to "conservation benefits." **[Sec. 2204]**
Duties of Producers	
Sec. 1240D(2) of the FSA, as amended, states that in exchange for EQIP payments, producers will not conduct any practices on the farm, ranch, or forest land that could defeat the purpose of the program. **[16 U.S.C. 3839aa-4(2)]**	Changes the practice restriction from "farm, ranch, or forest" land to "enrolled" land. **[Sec. 2205]**
Limitation on Payments	
Sec. 1240G of the FSA, as amended, limits EQIP participant's payments to $300,000 for any six-year period. This	Raises the EQIP payment limit to an aggregate of $450,000 between FY2014-FY2018 and eliminates the

Table A-3. (Continued)

Prior Law	Enacted 2014 Farm Bill (P.L. 113-79)
may be waived to up to $450,000 for any six-year period if the contract is of environmental significance. **[16 U.S.C. 3839aa-7]**	waiver authority for contracts of environmental significance. **[Sec. 2206]**
Conservation Innovation Grants (CIG)	
Sec. 1240H(a) of the FSA, as amended, authorizes Conservation Innovation Grants (CIG), a competitive grant program within EQIP. Grants are provided, on a matching basis, to implement innovative conservation practices. **[16 U.S.C. 3839aa-8(a)]**	Adds research and demonstration activities, and new technology pilot testing as eligible projects. **[Sec. 2207(1)]**
Sec. 1240H(b) of the FSA, as amended, provides $37.5 million of EQIP funds annually (FY2009-FY2013) to address air quality concerns. **[16 U.S.C. 3839aa-8(b)]**	Reauthorizes but reduces the air quality funding carve- out to $25 million of EQIP annually through FY2018. **[Sec. 2207(2)]**
No comparable provision	Adds a reporting requirement that no later than Dec. 31, 2014, and every two years thereafter, a report must be submitted to Congress regarding CIG funding, project results, and technology transfer efforts. **[Sec. 2207(3)]**
No comparable provision	Provides transition language stating that changes made by the 2014 farm bill do not affect the validity or terms of existing contracts. **[Sec. 2208]**
Funding	
Sec. 1241(a)(6) of the FSA, as amended, authorizes mandatory EQIP funding, rising from $1.2 billion in FY2008 to $1.622 billion in FY2015. **[16 U.S.C. 3841(a)(6)]**	Authorizes mandatory EQIP funding: $1.35 billion (FY2014); $1.6 billion (FY2015); $1.65 billion (FY2016-FY2017); and $1.75 billion (FY2018). Amended Sec. 1241(a)(5). **[Sec. 2601(a)]**

Source: CRS.

Notes: The enacted FY2014 appropriation (P.L. 113-76) reauthorized and amended EQIP. Because the changes were enacted prior to the enactment of the 2014 farm bill, they are reflected in the table as prior law.

Table A-4. Subtitle D—Agricultural Conservation Easement Program

Prior Law	Enacted 2014 Farm Bill (P.L. 113-79)
Establishment	
No directly comparable provision. Similar to the establishment and purposes section of the Wetlands Reserve Program (WRP, Sec. 1237(a)), the Farmland Protection Program (FPP, Sec. 1238I(a)&(b)), and the Grassland Reserve Program (GRP, Sec. 1238N(a)) of the Food Security Act of 1985 (FSA), as amended. **[16 U.S.C. 3837(a); 3838i(a)&(b); 3838n(a)]**	Establishes the Agricultural Conservation Easement Program (ACEP). Combines the purposes of WRP, FPP, and GRP. Amended Sec.1265of the Food Security Act of 1985 (FSA) **[Sec. 2301(a)]**
Definitions	
No directly comparable provision. Similar to definitions found in Sec. 1237 (WRP) and Sec. 1238H (FPP) of the FSA, as amended. **[16 U.S.C. 3837 & 3838h]**	Divides the easement program into two types—agricultural land easements (ALE), which include components of FPP and GRP; and wetland reserve easements (WRE), which include components of WRP. Defines the following: • **agricultural land easements**—an easement that protects the natural resources and the agricultural nature of the land, while maintaining production • **eligible entity**—an agency of state or local government, Indian tribe, or eligible organization • **eligible land**—separate for ALE and WRE. ALE includes land: with a pending ALE offer; with prime, unique, or productive soils; that contains historical or archaeological resources; that would protect grazing uses; that furthers a similar state or local policy; that is cropland, rangeland, grassland, area historically dominated by grassland, pastureland, or nonindustrial private forest land. WRE includes: farmed or converted wetlands; cropland

Table A-4. (Continued)

Prior Law	Enacted 2014 Farm Bill (P.L. 113-79)
	or grassland that has prior flooding from a closed basin lake or pothole if the state or other entity is willing to provide a 50% cost-share of the easement; wetlands enrolled in the CRP, have high wetland functions, and are likely to return to production after CRP; riparian areas that link protected wetlands; or wetlands determined by USDA to be significant. • **wetland reserve easement**—an easement defined and delineated in a deed that stipulates the rights, title, and interests in the land conveyed to USDA and reserved by the landowner Amended Sec. **1265A [Sec. 2301(a)]**
Agricultural Land Easements	
No directly comparable provision. Similar to Sec. 1238I (FPP) of the FSA, as amended. Provides for the purchase of conservation easements by limiting the land's nonagricultural uses. The federal cost may not exceed 50% of the appraised market value of the easement and entities must contribute a minimum of 25% of the acquisition purchase price. Prohibits bidding down (or choosing between similar projects based on lowest price). Requires USDA to include a contingent right of enforcement in the terms of the easement, and that a conservation plan be required for any easements that include highly erodible cropland. Establishes a certification process for USDA to enter into agreements. Entities must have the authority and	Retains much of the FPP easement requirements for costshare assistance, agreements with eligible entities, certification of eligible entities, including review and recertification requirements. Allows for grazing as a protected agricultural use, similar to GRP easements. Requires appraisals based on uniform standards of professional appraisal practice or any other industryapproved standard. Requires eligible entities to provide contributions equivalent to the federal share, or at least 50% of the federal share if the entity includes contributions from the private landowner. Allows up to 75% federal cost-share for grasslands of special environmental significance. Authorizes USDA to waive any portion of the eligible entity cash contribution requirement for projects of special significance, subject to an increase of private landowner donation equal to the

Prior Law	Enacted 2014 Farm Bill (P.L. 113-79)
resources to enforce easements, polices, and procedures. Agreements with certified entities are a minimum of five years with a review and recertification required every three years. Agreements with non-certified entities are three to five years in length. **[16 U.S.C. 3838i(c)-(h)]**	amount of the waiver if donation is voluntary. Establishes evaluation and ranking criteria for applications. All easements are permanent or for the maximum duration allowed under state law. Amended Sec. 1265B **[Sec. 2301(a)]**
Wetland Reserve Easements	
No directly comparable provision. Similar to Sec. 1237-1237F (WRP) of the FSA, as amended. WRP enrolls lands through the use of permanent easements, 30-year easements, restoration costshare agreements, or any combination thereof. Eligible lands under WRP include: farmed wetland or converted wetland, together with adjacent land, except wetlands converted before December 23, 1985; cropland or grassland that was used for agricultural production prior to flooding from the natural overflow of a closed basin lake or pothole; and possibly farmed wetlands enrolled in CRP that are likely to return to production upon contract expiration. Ineligible lands include CRP acres containing timber stands or CRP pasture established to trees. USDA is required to determine the value of easements and contracts by providing the lowest amount of compensation based on a comparison of the fair market value of the land, a geographic cap, or an offer made by the landowner. Easements with values less than $500,000 must be	Retains much of the WRP easement requirements for land eligibility, easement terms, compatible uses, easement compensation, violation procedures, duties of USDA and the owner, cost-share, restoration, and technical assistance requirements. Reauthorizes a program similar to WREP, referred to as the wetland enhancement option. No longer allows for stand-alone cost-share restoration agreements; only 30-year easements, permanent easements (or maximum duration allowed under law), and 30-year contracts for Indian Tribes, which may include restoration assistance. Reduces the land ownership requirement to the preceding 24-month period. Requires the establishment of an evaluation and ranking criteria that maximizes the benefit of federal investment. Retains priority for easements based on the value of protecting and enhancing habitat for migratory birds and other wildlife, but removes consideration for costs and future agricultural and food needs. Makes the reserved grazing rights pilot program permanent. Compensation provisions are similar to WRP, but adds a requirement that 30-year contract (Tribes only) and 30-year easement compensation be between 50% and 75% of a permanent

Table A-4. (Continued)

Prior Law	Enacted 2014 Farm Bill (P.L. 113-79)
paid out over 1-30 years; easements with values greater than $500,000 are to be paid out over 5-30 years. Authorized to conduct a Wetlands Reserve Enhancement Program (WREP) for agreements with states similar to CREP. Priority is given to easements based on the value of protecting and enhancing habitat for migratory birds and other wildlife, while taking into consideration costs and future agricultural and food needs. Eligible land cannot have changed ownership in the previous seven year period unless the new ownership was by will, succession, foreclosure, or USDA is assured the land was not acquired for the purpose of enrolling in WRP. **[16 U.S.C. 3837-3837f]**	easement's compensation. Payment schedules are changed for easements with values less than $500,000 to be paid out over not more than 10 years and easements with values greater than $500,000 to be paid out over 5-10 years. Restoration costshare is between 75%-100% for permanent easements and between 50%-75% for 30-year contracts (Tribes only) and 30-year easements. Easement administration may be delegated; however, the monitoring and enforcement responsibilities may not. Amended Sec. 1265C **[Sec. 2301(a)]**
Administration	
No directly comparable provision.	Outlines administrative requirements for ACEP using elements of WRP, FPP, and GRP. Land owned by the U.S. (not held in trust for Indian tribes), state, or local government is not eligible. The land may not be eligible if it currently has a similar easement or protection already in place or where the easement could be undermined by other conditions (e.g., hazardous substance, rights of way, etc.). Provides priority for expiring CRP acres to enter into (1) agricultural land easements if they are grasslands that would benefit from long-term easements, or (2) wetland easements, if they are wetlands with the highest functions and value that could return to production after leaving the

Prior Law	Enacted 2014 Farm Bill (P.L. 113-79)
	CRP. Allows the USDA to subordinate, exchange, modify, or terminate easements. Requires ACEP participants to meet highly erodible land and wetlands conservation (collectively known as conservation compliance) requirements. Amended Sec. 1265D. **[Sec. 2301(a)]**
Technical Amendments	
No directly comparable provision. Section 1244(f) of the FSA, as amended limits CRP and WRP enrollment to no more than 25% of a county's total cropland acreage. **[16 U.S.C. 3844 et seq.]**	Provides technical amendments for other sections. Excludes shelterbelts, windbreak, and wet and saturated soils from the 25% county acreage cap. Amends acreage limitations to include existing WRP acres in the 25% county acreage cap in addition to CRP and the new wetland easements under ACEP. **[Sec. 2301(b)]**
Funding	
No directly comparable provision. Sec. 1241(a)(2) and (a)(5) of the FSA, as amended, authorizes mandatory funding to enroll WRP & GRP acres respectively. Sec. 1241(a)(4) authorizes mandatory FPP funding, rising from $97 million in FY2008 to $200 million in FY2014. **[16 U.S.C. 3841(a)(2); (a)(4); (a)(5)]**	Authorizes mandatory ACEP funding: $400 million (FY2014); $425 million (FY2015); $450 million (FY2016); $500 million (FY2017); and $250 million (FY2018) Amended Sec. 1241(a)(2). **[Sec. 2601(a)]**

Source: CRS.

Table A-5. Subtitle E—Regional Conservation Partnership Program

Prior Law	Enacted 2014 Farm Bill (P.L. 113-79)
Purpose	
No directly comparable provision. Includes elements of the establishment and purposes section of the Agricultural Water Enhancement Program (AWEP, Sec. 1240I)), the Chesapeake Bay	Establishes the Regional Conservation Partnership Program (RCPP). Combines the purposes of AWEP, the Chesapeake Bay Watershed program, CCPI, and the Great Lakes basin program to further conservation,

Table A-5. (Continued)

Prior Law	Enacted 2014 Farm Bill (P.L. 113-79)
Watershed program (Sec. 1240Q), the Cooperative Conservation Partnership Initiative (CCPI, Sec. 1243) and the Great Lakes basin program for soil erosion and sediment control (Sec. 1240P) of the Food Security Act of 1985 (FSA), as amended. **[16 U.S.C. 3839aa-9; 3839bb-4; 3843; 3839bb-3]**	restoration, and sustainability on a regional or watershed scale, and encourage partners to cooperate with producers in meeting or avoiding regulatory requirements and implementing projects. Amended Sec. 1271 **[Sec. 2401]**
Definitions	
No directly comparable provision. Includes elements of the four consolidated programs.	Defines the following: • **covered program**—includes ACEP, EQIP, CSP, and HFRP • **eligible activities**—activities for water quality and quantity improvement, drought mitigation, flood prevention, water retention, air quality improvement, habitat conservation, erosion control and sediment reduction, forest restoration and others defined by USDA. • **eligible land**—cropland, grassland, rangeland, pastureland, nonindustrial private forest land, and other incidental land. • **eligible partner**—producer organizations, state or local governments, Indian tribes, farmer cooperatives, water districts, municipal water or waste treatment entity, institutes of higher education, and other nongovernmental entity or organizations with a history of working with producers on conservation projects. • **partnership agreement**—a regional conservation partnership agreement between an eligible partner and USDA. Amended Sec. 1271A **[Sec. 2401]**

Prior Law	Enacted 2014 Farm Bill (P.L. 113-79)
Regional Conservation Partnership	
No directly comparable provision. Includes elements of the consolidated programs, primarily AWEP and CCPI.	Authorizes competitive partnership agreements for a period not to exceed five years with a possible one-year extension. Describes the duties of partners as defining the scope of projects, conducting outreach, acting on behalf of producers to apply for assistance, leveraging financial and technical assistance, conducting assessments, and reporting results. Partners must provide a "significant portion" of the overall cost of the project. Applications are competitive and the selection criteria are publically available. Priority is given to applications that: assist producers meeting or avoiding the need for regulation; include a large percentage of producers in the project area; provide significant resource leverage; applies a high percentage of conservation to priorities or initiative; or provide innovative conservation methods and delivery. Amended Sec. 1271B **[Sec. 2401(a)]**
Assistance to Producers	
No directly comparable provision. Includes elements of the consolidated programs, primarily AWEP and CCPI.	Directs USDA to enter into contracts to provide technical and financial assistance to producers participating in projects with eligible partners, or producers within a project area or critical conservation area not working through an eligible partner. Program rules, requirements, and payments are to be consistent with the covered programs (ACEP, EQIP, & CSP). Provides USDA the authority to adjust the rules of a covered program, including operational guidance and requirements in order to simplify the application and evaluation process.

Table A-5. (Continued)

Prior Law	Enacted 2014 Farm Bill (P.L. 113-79)
	Prohibits the adjustment of statutory requirements for a covered program, including appeals, payment limits, conservation compliance, and prior irrigation history. Authorizes no more than 20 alternative funding arrangements with multi-state water agencies or authorities. Five year payments may be made for conversion to dryland farming and nutrient management. AGI limits may be waived to fulfill the objectives of the program. Amended Sec. 1271C **[Sec. 2401(a)]**
Funding	
No directly comparable provision. Sec. 1240I(j) of the FSA, as amended, authorizes mandatory AWEP funds of $73 million in FY2009 and FY2010, $74 million in FY2011, and $60 million each fiscal year thereafter. Sec. 1240Q(h) authorizes Chesapeake Bay Watershed program funds of $23 million in FY2009, $43 million in FY2010, $72 million in FY2011, and $50 million in FY2012. Sec. 1243(i) authorizes CCPI to use 6% of covered program for a state (90%) and national (10%) competition. Sec. 1240P(d) authorizes appropriations of $5 million annually for the Great Lakes basin program. **[16 U.S.C. 3839aa-9(j); 3838bb-4(h); 3843(i); 3839bb-3(d)]**	Authorizes $100 million annually for FY2014-FY2018 to remain available until expended. Similar to CCPI, the program utilizes a percentage of other conservation program funding. Annually reserves 7% of covered program funds and acres until April 1each year, after which time uncommitted funds are returned to the covered program. Allocates 25% for a state competition, 40% for a national competition, and 35% for critical conservation areas. Retains the AWEP and CCPI restriction on paying no administrative expenses of eligible partners. Amended Sec. 1271D **[Sec. 2401]**
Administration	
No comparable provision.	Requires USDA to make information on selected projects publicly available. Requires a report to Congress on

Prior Law	Enacted 2014 Farm Bill (P.L. 113-79)
	December 31, 2014 (and every two years thereafter) on the status of projects funded. Amended Sec. 1271E **[Sec. 2401(a)]**
Critical Conservation Areas	
No comparable provision.	Requires USDA to use 35% of the funds and acres available for partnership agreements in no more than eight critical conservation areas that expire after five years, subject to redesignation. Areas are selected based on: multi-state areas with significant agricultural production; existing agreement or plan in place; water quality concerns; water quantity concerns; or subject to regulatory requirements. Partner agreements and producer contracts are administered according to the applicable covered program and, where possible, complement existing water quality and quantity strategies. Allows the use of authorities granted under the Watershed Protection and Flood Prevention program in critical conservation areas. Amended Sec. 1271F **[Sec. 2401(a)]**

Source: CRS.

Table A-6. Subtitle F—Other Conservation Programs

Prior Law	Enacted 2014 Farm Bill (P.L. 113-79)
Sec. 1240M(e) of the Food Security Act of 1985 (FSA), as amended, authorizes the *Conservation of Private Grazing Land Program*. Authorizes appropriations of $60 million annually through FY2013. **[16 U.S.C, 3839bb(e)]**	Extends authorization of appropriations at $60 million annually through FY2018. **[Sec. 2501]**
Sec. 1240O(b) of the FSA, as amended, authorizes the *Grassroots Source Water*	Extends annual authorization of appropriations ($20 million)

Table A-6. (Continued)

Prior Law	Enacted 2014 Farm Bill (P.L. 113-79)
Protection Program. Authorizes appropriations of $20 million annually through FY2013. **[16 U.S.C. 3839bb-2(b)]**	through FY2018 and authorizes a one-time $5 million in mandatory funding from the Commodity Credit Corporation (CCC) to remain available until expended. **[Sec. 2502]**
Sec. 1240R of the FSA, as amended authorizes state grants through a *Voluntary Public Access and Habitat Incentive Program* to encourage landowners to provide public access for wildlife-dependent recreation. Sets application contents and award priorities providing $50 million in mandatory funds for the period for FY2013. **[16 U.S.C. 3839bb-5]**	Reduces and extends authorization of $40 million in mandatory funding for the period of FY2014-FY2018. Requires USDA to submit a report to Congress no later than two years after enactment on the effectiveness of the program. **[Sec. 2503]**
Sec. 1252 of FSA, as amended, authorizes an *Agriculture Conservation Experienced Service Program (ACES)*, such that USDA can enter into agreements with organizations to provide technical assistance (excludes administrative tasks) using qualified individuals 55 years or older. Funding from CRP, GRP, WRP, and CSP may not be used to carry out the ACES program. **[16 U.S.C. 3851]**	Allows funding for each conservation program in the Food Security Act of 1985, as amended, except CRP, to be used to carry out the ACES program. **[Sec. 2504]**
Sec. 14(h)(2)(E) of the Watershed Protection and Flood Prevention Act (P.L. 106-472), as amended, authorizes up to $85 million annually in discretionary funding for the *Small Watershed Rehabilitation Program* for FY2008- FY2013 and $100 million in mandatory funding for FY2009 to remain available until expended. **[16 U.S.C. 1012(h)(2)(E)]**	Extends authorization of appropriations through FY2018 and authorizes $250 million in mandatory funding for FY2014 to remain available until expended. **[Sec. 2505]**

Prior Law	Enacted 2014 Farm Bill (P.L. 113-79)
Sec. 403 of the Agricultural Credit Act of 1978 (P.L. 95- 334), as amended, authorizes USDA to assists sponsors, landowners, and operators in implementing emergency recovery measures for runoff retardation and erosion prevention to relieve imminent hazards to life and property created by a natural disaster under the *Emergency Watershed Protection Program*. This may include the purchase of floodplain easements. **[16 U.S.C.2203]**	Authorizes USDA to modify and terminate floodplain easements provided the current landowner agrees, and the modification or termination addresses a compelling public need for which there is no practical alternative, and is in the public interest. **[Sec. 2506]**
Sec. 2507 of the Food, Security and Rural Investment Act of 2002 (P.L. 107-171, 2002 farm bill), as amended, authorizes USDA to transfer $175 million of CCC funds to the Bureau of Reclamation to provide water for atrisk *desert terminal lakes*. **[43 U.S.C. 2211]**	Deletes current section and replaces with new section that adds definitions for eligible land, program, and terminal lake. Also adds a new voluntary land purchase grant program with authorization to receive $25 million through appropriations to remain available until expended. Retains provisions for voluntary water purchases for desert terminal lakes, including the transfer of $150 million of CCC funds to the Bureau of Reclamation. **[Sec. 2507]**
USDA is authorized and directed to develop in cooperation with and participation by the public through conservation districts, state and national organizations and agencies, and other appropriate means, a national *Soil and Water Conservation Program* to be used as a guide in carrying out the activities of USDA which assist landowners and land users, at their request, in furthering soil and water conservation on the private and nonfederal lands of the nation. **[16 U.S.C. 2005]**	Adds Indian tribes as being eligible to cooperate with and participate in the Soil and Water Conservation Program. **[Sec. 2508]**

Source: CRS.

Table A-7. Subtitle G—Funding and Administration

Prior Law	Enacted 2014 Farm Bill (P.L. 113-79)
Program Funding	
Sec. 1241(a) of the Food Security Act of 1985 (FSA), as amended, authorizes the use of funds (mandatory), facilities, and authorities of the Commodity Credit Corporation (CCC) to carry out conservation programs between FY2002 through FY2012 (through FY2014 and FY2015 for select programs). **[16 U.S.C. 3841(a)]**	Deletes current section and replaces with new section that extends the CCC authority between FY2014 and FY2018. Specific funding levels for programs are outlined below. **[Sec. 2601(a)]**
Sec. 1241(a)(1) of the FSA, as amended, authorizes CCC (mandatory funding) to carry out CRP for FY2002- FY2012. Specifically authorizes $100 million for thinning activities and $25 million for transition contracts between FY2009-FY2012. Total funding for CRP is limited by enrolled acres, not total dollars. See Table A- 1. **[16 U.S.C. 3841(a)(1)]**	Reauthorizes the authority for CCC to carry out CRP between FY2014 and FY2018. Specifically authorizes $10 million for thinning incentive payments and $33 million for transition contracts. **[Sec. 2601(a)]**
Sec. 1241(a)(2) of the FSA, as amended, authorizes the CCC (mandatory funding) to carry out WRP for FY2002-FY2012. Total funding for WRP is limited by enrolled acres, not total dollars. **[16 U.S.C. 3841(a)(2)]**	Removes the WRP authority and replaces with an authorization for ACEP: $400 million (FY2014); $425 million (FY2015); $450 million (FY2016); $500 million (FY2017); and $250 million (FY2018). See Table A-4. **[Sec. 2601(a)]**
Sec. 1241(a)(3) of the FSA, as amended, authorizes the CCC (mandatory funding) to carry out CSP for FY2002- FY2014. Total funding for CSP is limited by enrolled acres, not total dollars. Allows Conservation Security Program contracts (enrolled prior to FY2009) to be paid with mandatory funding. **[16 U.S.C. 3841(a)(3)]**	Reauthorizes the authority for CCC to carry out CSP between FY2014 and FY2018. **[Sec. 2601(a)]**

Prior Law	Enacted 2014 Farm Bill (P.L. 113-79)
Sec. 1241(a)(4) of the FSA, as amended, authorizes the CCC to carry out FPP for FY2002-FY2014: $97 million (FY2008); $121 million (FY2009); $150 million (FY2010); $175 million (FY2011); and $200 million (FY2012- FY2014). **[16 U.S.C. 3841(a)(4)]**	Removes the FPP authority and replaces with an authorization for ACEP: $400 million (FY2014); $425 million (FY2015); $450 million (FY2016); $500 million (FY2017); and $250 million (FY2018). See Table A-4. **[Sec. 2601(a)]**
Sec. 1241(a)(5) of the FSA, as amended, authorizes the CCC (mandatory funding) to carry out GRP for FY2002- FY2012. Total funding for GRP is limited by enrolled acres, not total dollars. **[16 U.S.C. 3841(a)(5)]**	Removes the GRP authority and replaces with an authorization for ACEP: $400 million (FY2014); $425 million (FY2015); $450 million (FY2016); $500 million (FY2017); and $250 million (FY2018). See Table A-4. **[Sec. 2601(a)]**
Sec. 1241(a)(6) of the FSA, as amended, authorizes the CCC (mandatory funding) to carry out EQIP for FY2002- FY2015: $1.2 billion (FY2008); $1.337 billion (FY2009); $1.45 billion (FY2010); $1.588 billion (FY2011); $1.75 billion (FY2012-FY2014); and $1.622 billion (FY2015). **[16 U.S.C. 3841(a)(6)]**	Reauthorizes the authority for CCC to carry out EQIP between FY2014-FY2018: $1.35 billion (FY2014); $1.6 billion (FY2015); $1.65 billion (FY2016-FY2017); and $1.75 billion (FY2018). **[Sec. 2601(a)]**
Sec. 1241(a)(7) of the FSA, as amended, authorizes the CCC to carry out WHIP for FY2002-FY2014: $15 million (FY2002); $30 million (FY2003); $60 million (FY2004); and $85 million (FY2005-FY2014). **[16 U.S.C. 3841(a)(7)]**	Removes WHIP authority. Requires a minimum of 5% of annual EQIP funds go to payments benefiting wildlife habitat through FY2018. See Table A-3. **[Sec. 2203(4)]**
No comparable provision.	Allows mandatory funding made available for CRP, ACEP, CSP, and EQIP to remain available until expended. **[Sec. 2601(b)]**
Use of Program Funds	
Sec. 1241(c) of the FSA, as amended, allows CCC funds for conservation programs to also be used for technical assistance. **[16 U.S.C. 3841(b)]**	Allows CCC (mandatory) funds for conservation programs to also be used for technical assistance, with the exception of CRP, which is at the discretion of USDA.

Table A-7. (Continued)

Prior Law	Enacted 2014 Farm Bill (P.L. 113-79)
	Requires USDA to give priority to producers who request technical assistance to comply with highly erodible land conservation (sodbuster) and wetland conservation (swampbuster) for the first time because of the changes made under Sec. 2611 (ties crop insurance subsidies to compliance requirements, discussed further below). Requires a report to Congress in 270 days after enactment on the impact conservation compliance has on specialty crop growers. Requires a report to Congress by December 31, 2013 (and each subsequent year), detailing the amount of technical assistance requested and apportioned for each conservation program. Requires an annual report to Congress on November 1 each year describing how conservation compliance is being addressed in a timely manner, total requests completed, incomplete determinations on record, and requests older than a year. **[Sec. 2602]**
Sec. 1241(d) of the FSA, as amended, requires that each state receives an aggregated minimum of $15 million annually from certain mandatory conservation programs in order to promote regional equity. **[16 U.S.C. 3841(d)]**	Eliminates the $15 million annual minimum and allows states in the first quarter of the fiscal year to establish that they can use a total of 0.6% of certain conservation funds. If established, those states may receive 0.6% of funds. **[Sec. 2603]**
Sec. 1241(g) of the FSA, as amended, establishes an annual set-aside in EQIP and CSP from FY2009-FY2013; 5% to beginning farmers or ranchers and 5% to socially	Reauthorizes the EQIP and CSP set-aside through FY2018. Provides preference for veteran farmers or ranchers eligible under the provision. **[Sec. 2604]**

Prior Law	Enacted 2014 Farm Bill (P.L. 113-79)
disadvantaged farmers or ranchers. **[16 U.S.C. 3841(g)]**	
Sec. 1241(h) of the FSA, as amended, establishes reporting requirements for program enrollments and assistance under WRP, FPP, GRP, EQIP, AWEP, CSP, and adjusted gross income waivers. **[16 U.S.C. 3841(h)]**	Amends reporting requirements to reflect the repeal of WRP, FPP, GRP, and AWEP and the addition of ACEP and RCPP. Adds reporting requirements for CSP payments and waivers granted to grasslands under ACEP. **[Sec. 2605]**
Administrative Provisions	
Sec. 1244 of the FSA, as amended, outlines administrative requirements for conservation programs including incentives for certain farmers or ranchers, privacy information, conservation plans, acreage limitations, and applications, among others. **[16 U.S.C. 3844]**	Adds veteran farmers and ranchers to the list of eligible persons authorized to receive incentives. Makes conforming amendments to reflect the new ACEP program. Encourages streamlining and technology use to enhance efficiency and effectiveness. Clarifies that conservation payments are in addition to and not included in any payment limit caps. Allows for flexible funding arrangements for Indian Tribes and includes EQIP and CSP as applicable programs. **[Sec. 2606]**
Sec. 1261(b) of the FSA, as amended, requires USDA to develop standard committee operating procedures for State Technical Committees. **[16 U.S.C. 3861(b)]**	Amends provision to allow USDA to review and update standards as necessary. **[Sec. 2607]**
Sec. 2904 of the Food, Conservation, and Energy Act of 2008, (P.L. 110-246, 2008 farm bill) requires USDA, in consultation with CCC, to issue rules and regulations implementing Title II provisions within 90 days. Waives certain rulemaking requirements.	Amends and adds the 2008 farm bill regulations provision to a new Sec. 1246 of the FSA. Allows interim final rules to be effective upon issuance and waives the Paperwork Reduction Act requirements (44 U.S.C. 35). **[Sec. 2608]**
Compliance Requirements and Reports	
Sec. 1222 of the FSA, as amended, allows USDA to exempt persons from	Adds language that amends Sec. 1222(k) of the FSA, authorizing

Table A-7. (Continued)

Prior Law	Enacted 2014 Farm Bill (P.L. 113-79)
ineligibility under wetland compliance (swampbuster) if certain factors exist, including: there is a minimal effect; the values, functions, and acreage are mitigated; conversion occurred after December 23, 1985, but before November 28, 1990, and are mitigated; or the action is authorized by a Clean Water Act section 404 permit (33 U.S.C. 1344). Sec. 1222(k) of the FSA, as amended, allowed USDA to operate a pilot program for mitigation banking. **[16 U.S.C. 3822]**	USDA to expand and make permanent the wetland mitigation banking pilot program. Provides $10 million mandatory funding to remain available until expended. Allows access to existing mitigation banks. **[Sec. 2609]**
No comparable provision.	Requires a report to Congress 90 days after enactment reviewing the activities that apply to the lesser prairie- chicken under: CRP; EQIP; the Lesser Prairie-Chicken Initiative; the Western Association of Fish and Wildlife Agencies Candidate Conservation Agreement with Assurances for Oil and Gas; and the Western Association of Fish and Wildlife Agencies Lesser Prairie-Chicken Range-Wide Conservation Plan. **[Sec. 2610]**
Sec. 1211 of the FSA, as amended, requires that in exchange for certain USDA program benefits, a producer agrees to maintain a minimum level of conservation on highly erodible land (referred to as HEL compliance). Examples of affected benefit include commodity support programs (e.g., Title I farm bill programs), conservation programs, disaster payments, and operating loans. **[16 U.S.C. 3811]**	Adds the federally funded portion of crop insurance premiums to the list of program benefits that could be lost if a producer is found to produce an agricultural commodity on highly erodible land without an approved conservation plan or qualifying exemption. **[Sec. 2611(a)(1)]**
Sec. 1212 of the FSA, as amended, allows producers to cultivate crops on	Provides a separate provision for crop insurance benefits. A person subject

Prior Law	Enacted 2014 Farm Bill (P.L. 113-79)
highly erodible land and remain eligible for program benefits if the landowner agrees to cultivate the land using an approved conservation plan or qualifies for an exemption. **[16 U.S.C. 3812]**	to compliance for the first time because of these amendments is given five reinsurance years to develop and comply with an approved conservation plan to remain eligible for payments. A person who would have been determined in violation had they continued participation in programs requiring compliance after enactment of this bill and are still in violation must be granted two reinsurance years to develop and comply with an approved conservation plan. A person found in violation during a crop year shall be ineligible for crop insurance payment. This applies to reinsurance years subsequent to the date of the final determination of a violation and does not apply to the existing reinsurance year or any reinsurance year prior to the date of the final determination. **[Sec. 2611(a)(2)]**
Sec. 1213 of the FSA, as amended, outlines the requirements for development and implementation of conservation plans for conservation compliance. **[16 U.S.C. 3812a]**	Requires that when determining crop insurance premium assistance, USDA must allow self-certification of compliance and act in a timely manner to evaluate such certifications, as well as avoid duplication or unnecessary paperwork. **[Sec. 2611(a)(3)]**
Sec. 1221 et seq. of the FSA, as amended, requires that in exchange for certain USDA program benefits, a producer agrees not to convert wetlands to crop production. The provision, known as Swampbuster, affects producers who plant a program crop on a wetland converted after December 23, 1985, or who convert wetlands, making agricultural commodity production possible, after	Adds the federally funded portion of crop insurance premiums to the list of program benefits that could be lost if a producer is found to have converted a wetland to crop production. Persons in violation who meet select criteria have a varying amount of time (one to two reinsurance years) to initiate a conservation plan to remedy a violation and remain eligible. Requires an annual report on

Table A-7. (Continued)

Prior Law	Enacted 2014 Farm Bill (P.L. 113-79)
November 28, 1990. Examples of affected benefits include commodity support programs (e.g., Title I farm bill programs), conservation programs, disaster payments, and operating loans. **[16 U.S.C. 3821 et seq.]**	ineligibility determinations. All persons applying for the federally funded portion of crop insurance in the first full reinsurance year after enactment must certify their compliance with the wetlands compliance provision. USDA must evaluate the certifications in a timely manner. A person found in violation is only declared ineligible following final determination and may not be retroactive. The timing of a violation affects eligibility. Only USDA is responsible for the enforcement of compliance. **[Sec. 2611(b)(2)]**

Source: CRS.

Notes: Authorized funding levels for various programs are provided in individual program tables as well as this table.

Table A-8. Subtitle H—Program Repeals, Transition Provisions, and Technical Amendments

Prior Law	Enacted 2014 Farm Bill (P.L. 113-79)
Program Repeals	
Sec. 1230 of the Food Security Act of 1985 (FSA), as amended, authorizes and establishes the comprehensive conservation enhancement program between FY1996- FY2002. **[16 U.S.C. 3830]**	Repeals the comprehensive conservation enhancement program. **[Sec. 2701]**
Sec. 1231A of the FSA, as amended, authorizes and establishes the emergency forestry conservation reserve program within CRP for areas suffering damage during the CY2005 hurricanes. **[16 U.S.C. 3831a]**	Repeals the emergency forestry conservation reserve program with transition provisions for current contracts to receive CRP funding until expiration. **[Sec. 2702]**
Sec. 1237-1237F of the FSA, as amended, authorizes and establishes	Repeals WRP with transition provisions for current contracts and

Prior Law	Enacted 2014 Farm Bill (P.L. 113-79)
the Wetlands Reserve Program (WRP). **[16 U.S.C. 3837-3837f]**	easements to receive CCC funding until expiration. ACEP funding may also be used. **[Sec. 2703]**
Sec. 1238H-1238J of the FSA, as amended, authorizes and establishes the Farmland Protection Program (FPP) and the Farm Viability Program. **[16 U.S.C. 3838h- 3838j]**	Repeals FPP with transition provisions for current agreements and easements to receive CCC funding until expiration. ACEP funding may also be used once prior year funding is exhausted. Also repeals the Farm Viability Program. **[Sec. 2704]**
Sec. 1238N-1238P of the FSA, as amended, authorizes and establishes the Grasslands Reserve Program (GRP). **[16 U.S.C. 3838n-3838p]**	Repeals GRP with transition provisions for current contracts, agreements, and easements to receive CCC funding until expiration. ACEP funding may also be used. **[Sec. 2705]**
Sec. 1240I of the FSA, as amended, authorizes and establishes the Agricultural Water Enhancement Program (AWEP) within EQIP. **[16 U.S.C. 3839aa-9]**	Repeals AWEP with transition provisions for current contracts and agreements to receive CCC funding until expiration. RCPP funding may also be used once prior year funding is exhausted. **[Sec. 2706]**
Sec. 1240N of the FSA, as amended, authorizes and establishes the Wildlife Habitat Incentives Program (WHIP). **[16 U.S.C. 3839bb-1]**	Repeals WHIP with transition provisions for current contracts to receive CCC funding until expiration. EQIP funding may also be used once prior year funding is exhausted. **[Sec. 2707]**
Sec. 1240P of the FSA, as amended, authorizes and establishes the Great Lakes Basin Program for Soil Erosion and Sediment Control. **[16 U.S.C. 3839bb-3]**	Repeals the Great Lakes basin program. **[Sec. 2708]**
Sec. 1240Q of the FSA, as amended, authorizes and establishes the Chesapeake Bay Watershed program. **[16 U.S.C. 3839bb-4]**	Repeals the Chesapeake Bay Watershed program with transition provisions for current contracts, agreements, and easements entered into under the program to receive CCC funding until expiration. RCPP funding may also be used. **[Sec. 2709]**

Table A-8. (Continued)

Prior Law	Enacted 2014 Farm Bill (P.L. 113-79)
Sec. 1243 of the FSA, as amended, authorizes and establishes the Cooperative Conservation Partnership Initiative (CCPI). **[16 U.S.C. 3843]**	Repeals CCPI with transition provisions for current contracts and agreements to receive CCC funding until expiration. RCPP funding may also be used once prior year funding is exhausted. **[Sec. 2710]**
Sec. 1239-1239D of the FSA, as amended, authorizes and establishes the environmental easement program between CY1991-CY1995. **[16 U.S.C. 3839-3839d]**	Repeals the environmental easement program. **[Sec. 2711]**
Transition Provision	
No comparable provision.	Adds a new section to address the multiple effective dates within Title II. Grants USDA 270 days after enactment to continue using existing regulations to implement new and amended programs in the absence of new regulations. **[Sec. 2712]**
No comparable provision.	Provides technical amendments and spelling corrections. **[Sec. 2713]**

Source: CRS.

End Notes

[1] All farm bill conservation programs are administered by the U.S. Department of Agriculture's (USDA's) Natural Resources Conservation Service (NRCS), with the exception of the Conservation Reserve Program (CRP), which is administered by USDA's Farm Service Agency (FSA).

[2] Letter from Douglas W. Elmendorf, Director, CBO, to Honorable Frank D. Lucas, Chairman House Committee on Agriculture, January 28, 2014, http://www.cbo.gov/publication/45049. The CBO baseline is an estimate (projection) at a particular point in time of what future federal spending on mandatory programs would be under current law.

[3] The other two titles reduced in the 2014 farm bill were Nutrition (Title IV) and Commodities (Title I).

[4] The House-passed farm bill (H.R. 2642) would have reduced Title II funding by $4.83 billion over 10 years, compared to the Senate-passed farm bill (S. 954), which proposed a reduction of $3.51 billion over 10 years.

[5] The projected impact of sequestration was released by CBO in the May 2013 baseline for farm bill programs, and the 2013 scores of the House and Senate farm bill proposals. For more information, see CRS Report R42484, *Budget Issues That Shaped the 2014 Farm Bill.*

[6] 7 U.S.C. 1524(b).

[7] Additional information about CRP may be found in CRS Report R42783, *Conservation Reserve Program (CRP): Status and Issues.*

[8] Further explained in CRS Report R41433, *Expiring Farm Bill Programs Without a Budget Baseline.*

[9] Further explained in CRS Report R42442, *Expiration and Extension of the 2008 Farm Bill.*

[10] Certified entities are defined in statute as having a plan for administering easements that is consistent with the purposes of the program, the capacity and resources to enforce and monitor easements, and policies and procedures to protect the integrity of the easements and complete timely acquisitions and evaluations of such easements.

[11] The value may be determined using the Uniform Standards of Professional Appraisal Practice, an area-wide market analysis or survey, or another industry-approved method.

[12] Permanent easements are eligible for not less than 75% and not more than 100% of the restoration costs. 30-year contracts and 30-year easements are eligible for not less than 50% and not more than 75% of the restoration costs.

[13] Compensation is based on the lowest of: 1) the fair market value, 2) a geographical cap determined by USDA, or 3) the offer made by the landowner.

[14] Thirty-year contracts or 30-year easements may not be less than 50%, or more than 75% of the compensation for a permanent easement.

[15] The GLBP was last funded as a congressional directive (earmark) in FY2010 for a total of $404,000. Funds directly supported the Great Lakes Commission and local conservation priorities in the Great Lakes region. Funding was terminated in the FY2011 short-term continuing resolution (P.L. 112-4), which said that all FY2010 earmarks, "have no legal effect." Ultimately, the Natural Resources Conservation Service (NRCS) terminated funding for the GLBP and has not entered into any new agreements since. While funds were no longer provided to the Commission, NRCS began redirecting other conservation program funding to the Great Lakes region as part of a larger Great Lakes Restoration Initiative, which includes 11 federal agencies. For more information, see http://greatlakesrestoration.us/index.html.

[16] In addition to the covered programs' authority, RCPP may also use authority under the Watershed Protection and Flood Prevention Act (referred to as Watershed and Flood Prevention Operations (WFPO), 16 U.S.C. 1001 et seq.) for water quantity improvement projects within a CCA. For additional information on WFPO projects, see CRS Report RL30478, *Federally Supported Water Supply and Wastewater Treatment Programs.*

[17] For additional information on how conservation compliance works, see CRS Report R42459, *Conservation Compliance and U.S. Farm Policy.*

[18] 7 U.S.C. 1501 et seq.

[19] In 2013, an average of 62% of the total crop insurance premium was paid for by the federal government, and the remainder by the participating farmer.

[20] Reinsurance year is a 12-month period that begins on July 1st. For additional information about the federal crop insurance program, see CRS Report R40532, *Federal Crop Insurance: Background.*

[21] Examples of exempt wetlands include a wetland converted to cropland before enactment of the 1985 farm bill (December 23, 1985), artificially created lakes, ponds, or wetlands, and wetlands created by irrigation delivery systems. A full list of exempt lands may be found in CRS Report R42459, *Conservation Compliance and U.S. Farm Policy.*

[22] 16 U.S.C. 3822(f).

[23] 16 U.S.C. 3822(f).

[24] For more information on crop insurance and NAP, see CRS Report R40532, *Federal Crop Insurance: Background* and CRS Report RS21212, *Agricultural Disaster Assistance.*

[25] Section 11014.

[26] For example, a 50 percentage point reduction would lower a premium subsidy rate of 62% to 12%. In 2013, an average of 62% of the total crop insurance premium was paid for by the federal government, and the remainder by the participating farmer.

In: Conservation Provisions ...
Editor: Arianna R. Hills

ISBN: 978-1-61122-559-4

Chapter 2

CONSERVATION RESERVE PROGRAM (CRP): STATUS AND ISSUES*

Megan Stubbs

SUMMARY

The Conservation Reserve Program (CRP) provides payments to agricultural producers to take highly erodible and environmentally sensitive land out of production and install resource conserving practices for 10 or more years. CRP was first authorized in the Food SecurityAct of 1985 (P.L. 99-198, 1985 farm bill) and is administered by the U.S. Department ofAgriculture's (USDA) Farm Service Agency (FSA) with technical support from other USDA agencies. Participants offer land for enrollment through two types of sign-up: general and continuous. General sign-ups are competitive and only open during select times. Continuous sign-ups are not competitive, always open for enrollment, and offer additional financial incentives to those who qualify.

Continuous sign-ups are targeted to specific environmental and resource concerns and operate through a number of initiatives. The largest and most well known is the Conservation Reserve Enhancement Program (CREP), which partners with states to address agricultural-related environmental

* This is an edited, reformatted and augmented version of a Congressional Research Service publication R42783, prepared for Members and Committees of Congress dated March 18, 2013.

concerns in specific geographic regions. While the majority of current acres enrolled were under general sign-ups (21.5 million acres), an increasing number are enrolled under continuous sign-ups (5.4 million acres).

Program and funding authority for CRP was extended in the American Taxpayer Relief Act (P.L. 112-240) and will now expire on September 30, 2013. Without reauthorization or an extension of authority the agency cannot approve any contracts or process any offers for enrollment. Congress continues to debate the reauthorization or extension of the 2008 farm bill, which authorized CRP to enroll up to 32 million acres. Bills considered, but not enacted, in the 112th Congress would reduce the authorized number of acres to 25 million and reauthorize the program through FY2017.

A number of factors have impacted CRP enrollment recently, mainly high commodity crop prices. These high crop prices have increased demand to put CRP acres back into production, even marginal acres. This pressure could potentially reduce the number of CRP acres offered for reenrollment once they have expired or cause existing current CRP participants to seek an early release from their CRP contract. Some participants also have cited a potentially low CRP rental rate compared to the market rental rate as a reason for decreased enrollment interest. Despite these factors, enrollment has increased under continuous sign-ups and demand for the program, in general, still exceeds the enrollment cap.

CRP has contributed to a number of environmental benefits including reduced soil erosion, improved water quality through wetlands and field buffers, reduced fertilizer use, and increased wildlife habitat. The recent expiration of a number of acres from the program, and a reduced reenrollment, has some concerned that a number of the environmental benefits gained under CRP could be lost or reduced if land is returned to production.

The Conservation Reserve Program (CRP) is the largest federal, private-land retirement program in the United States. The program provides financial compensation for landowners to voluntarily remove land from agricultural production for an extended period (typically 10 to 15 years) for the benefit of soil and water quality improvement and wildlife habitat.

The program was first authorized in the Food SecurityAct of 1985 (1985 farm bill, P.L. 99-198), initially as both a supply management tool for removing land from agricultural production, thus lowering commodity supply and potentially raising prices, and for providing environmental benefits. Currently over 27 million acres are enrolled in the program with total funding of close to $2 billion annually.

Acres enrolled in CRP have shown a number of positive environmental benefits including reduced soil erosion; water quality improvements through vegetative cover, buffer strips, and reduced fertilizer application; and wildlife population improvement from increased habitat. While a number of natural resource improvements are attributed to the program, the program contains a number of controversial elements as well, including the economic and environmental effect of haying and grazing on CRP acres; the expiration of program authority; and the early termination of contracts and reduced enrollment due to high crop prices.

Program and funding authority for CRP expires September 30, 2013, and reauthorization or another possible extension is being debated by Congress as part of the larger farm bill reauthorization debate.

How CRP Works

The program is administered by the Farm Service Agency (FSA) at the U.S. Department of Agriculture (USDA), with technical support from the Natural Resources Conservation Service (NRCS) and other USDA agencies.

Enrollment

In total, no more than 32 million acres may be enrolled in CRP at any given time. There are two main types of enrollment into CRP: general sign-up and continuous sign-up. Several continuous sign-up "initiatives" focus enrollment on specific resource concerns or conservation practices.

General Sign-Up

CRP is a competitive program, in which landowners offer eligible land for enrollment into the program. A general sign-up is a specific period of time during which FSA accepts these offers. Offers are ranked according to an Environmental Benefits Index (EBI, see text box) to determine the relative environmental benefits for the land offered.

For each general sign-up, FSA collects data on each of the EBI factors and ranks all eligible offers across the country. After the sign-up ends, USDA determines an EBI threshold. Acceptance for enrollment into CRP is extended to offers that scored above the EBI threshold. This threshold varies by sign-up depending on the offers received. Producers generally try to maximize EBI points and increase the likelihood that their offer will be accepted for enrollment. As of February 2013, 21.5 million acres were enrolled in CRP under general sign-up contracts, or 80% of total CRP acres. This includes 291,395 contracts on 195,061 farms.[2] During the most recent general sign-up (#43), 4.5 million acres were offered for enrollment and 3.9 million acres were accepted. On February 16, 2013, USDA announced that CRP general sign-up #45 will be held from May 20, 2013, through June 14, 2013. General sign-up contracts are effective on October 1 of the next fiscal year.

Continuous Sign-Up

Continuous sign-up is designed to enroll the most environmentally desirable land into CRP through specific conservation practices or resource needs. Unlike the general sign-up process, land offered under continuous sign-up may be enrolled at any time and is not subject to competitive bidding. If offers meet certain eligibility requirements then they are automatically accepted. Contracts are effective the first day of the month following the month of approval and typically include additional financial incentives.

ENVIRONMENTAL BENEFIT INDEX (EBI)

Following the 1990 farm bill (P.L. 101-624), CRP was required to consider the environmental benefits of the land offered for enrollment. The formulation of the EBI has changed over time, including becoming more transparent to participants.

Generally, the EBI is a standardized way to compare different land types with different resource needs across the country. The EBI is designed to compare the benefits that offered land can provide.

Presently, FSA collects data for each of the EBI factors for the land offered. These factors are weighted and scored based on the land's potential to generate the desired environmental benefits. Some factors are made up of sub-factors (listed in parentheses).

The current general sign-up (#45) will include the following factors and weights:[1]

- **Wildlife Factor** evaluates the expected wildlife benefits of the offer (wildlife habitat cover benefits, wildlife enhancement, and wildlife priority zones)— *10-100 points*

- **Water Quality Benefits Factor** evaluates the potential impact that the offer may have on both ground and surface water quality (location, ground water quality, and surface water quality)— *0-100 points*
- **Erosion Factor** evaluates the potential for the land to erode from wind or water and is measured using an erodibility index— *0-100 points*
- **Enduring Benefits Factor** evaluates the likelihood for certain practices to remain in place beyond the CRP contract period (weighted average for all practices)— *0-50 points*
- **Air Quality Benefits Factor** evaluates the air quality improvements made by reduced particulate matter and increased carbon sequestration (wind erosion impacts, wind erosion soils list, air quality zones, and carbon sequestered)— *3-45 points*
- **Cost** of environmental benefits per dollar expended (cost of the offer and how much the offer is below the maximum payment rate)— *0-25 points.*

Continuous sign-up includes a number of initiatives that target acres with specific resource concerns or support additional conservation practices. These are described in the Appendix.

As of February 2013, 5.5 million acres were enrolled in CRP under continuous sign-up, or 20% of total CRP acres. This includes 1.6 million enrolled through the two statutorily created sub-programs—the Conservation Reserve Enhancement Program (CREP, 1.3 million acres) and farmable wetlands (341,176 acres).[3]

The remaining 3.8 million acres were enrolled in other continuous sign-up initiatives.

Eligibility

Producer/Landowner

To be eligible for CRP enrollment, a producer must be an owner, operator, or tenant of the land for at least 12 months prior to the close of the CRP sign-up period, and show control of the land for the duration of the contract. The land may be eligible if owned for less than 12 months and if (1) the land was acquired due to the previous owner's death; (2) the ownership change occurred due to foreclosure where the owner exercised a timely right of redemption in accordance with state law; or (3) adequate assurances are made that the new owner did not acquire the land for the purpose of placing it in CRP.[4]

Land

For land to be eligible for CRP, USDA may consider the following land types for enrollment:[5]

- highly erodible cropland that (1) if untreated could substantially reduce the land's future agricultural production capability or (2) cannot be farmed in accordance with a conservation plan;[6] and has a cropping history or was considered to be planted for four of the six years between 2002-2007 (except for land previously enrolled in CRP);
- marginal pasture land converted to wetland or established as wildlife habitat prior to November 28, 1990, or devoted to appropriate vegetation or water quality purposes;
- cropland that is otherwise ineligible, if it is determined that (1) if permitted to remain in agricultural production, it would contribute to the degradation of soil, water, or air quality; (2) the land is a newly-created, permanent grass sod waterway, or a contour grass sod strip; (3) the land will be devoted to newly established living snow fences, permanent wildlife habitat, windbreaks, shelterbelts, or filterstrips devoted to trees or shrubs; (4) the land poses an off-farm environmental threat; or (5) enrollment of the land would facilitate a net savings in groundwater or surface water resources; or
- certain land enrolled as a riparian buffer or for similar water quality purposes.

Payments

In exchange for enrollment into CRP, participants receive payments from USDA. These payments offset the cost of temporarily retiring the land from production and implementing resource-conserving and wildlife-promoting practices.

A number of payment types under CRP are highlighted in Table 1.

Table 1. CRP Payments

Payment Type	Description	Limit	Sign-up Type
Rental Payment	Annual payment to participants. Based on soil productivity for each county and the average dryland case rental rate.	$50,000 annually for any person or legal entity	general and continuous sign-up
Cost-share Payment	Payment for a percentage of installing or establishing an eligible practice.	No more than 50% of the actual or average cost of establishing the practice.	general and continuous sign-up
Maintenance Incentive Payment	Reimburses participants for the average annual cost of certain practice maintenance.	$5 per acre per year	certain continuous sign-up practices
One-time Sign-up Incentive Payment (SIP)	One-time incentive payment made to participants that enroll certain practices.	$10 per acre per year enrolled (not to exceed 10 years)	certain continuous sign-up practices.
One-time Practice Incentive Payment (PIP)	One-time incentive payment for eligible installation costs for certain practices	40% of the eligible cost of practice installation	certain continuous sign-up practices.
Other Financial Incentive	Additional incentives, as part of annual rental payments, for windbreaks, grass waterways, filter strips, and riparian buffers	Up to 20% of the annual rental payment	certain continuous sign-up practices.

Sources: 16 U.S.C. 3834, 7 C.F.R. 1410.40-1410.42, and USDA, FSA, *Conservation Reserve Program Continuous Sign-Up*, Fact Sheet, July 2010, http://www.fsa.usda.gov/Internet/FSA_File/crp_contsignup_072610.pdf.

The authorizing statute establishes the maximum number of acres that can be enrolled in the program at any one time.[7] The program is authorized to spend such sums as necessary to enroll up to the maximum level of allowable acres. This funding is mandatory (i.e., not subject to annual appropriations) and is provided through the borrowing authority of the USDA's Commodity

Credit Corporation (CCC). In total, the average annual federal cost for CRP is close to $2 billion. The majority of this cost is annual rental payments, which averages $60.84 per acre, but can vary greatly by location.[8]

Practices

Producers have a number of conservation practices to consider for installation on their land when enrolling in CRP. The selection of practices is part of the voluntary enrollment process and is determined by the landowner, with assistance from USDA, while developing a CRP offer. Once an offer is accepted for enrollment, the participant must develop a conservation plan of operation, which serves as a guide for which practices will be used, where, and for how long. Once the plan is approved and the contract signed by the participant, the land is considered enrolled in CRP. Certain continuous sign-up initiatives require specific conservation practices for enrollment. The most widely applied conservation practices are described in Table 2.

CURRENT ISSUES

Farm Bill Expiration, Extension, and Reauthorization

The 2008 farm bill (P.L. 110-246) authorized CRP (both program and funding) to operate until September 30, 2012. The program was extended at its current level to September 30, 2013, in the American Taxpayer Relief Act of 2012 (P.L. 112-240). Without program and funding authority USDA cannot enroll any additional acres into the program. Contracts in place before September 30, 2013, will receive payments, including incentive payments, and will continue to be enforced. Without reauthorization or another extension of authority the agency cannot approve any contracts or process any offers for enrollment. While all sign-up types are affected by the lack of program and funding authority, continuous sign-up acres could be more impacted than general sign-ups in the short-term because acres are usually enrolled year-round.

The 112th Congress debated the reauthorization of many farm bill programs, including CRP. Both the Senate-passed (S. 3240) and House Agriculture Committee-reported (H.R. 6083) versions of the 2012 farm bill would have reauthorized CRP through FY2017. Both versions would also have incrementally reduced the maximum enrollable acres from 32 million to 25 million. According to the Congressional Budget Office (CBO), this reduction would have saved between $3.6 billion and $3.8 billion over ten years, compared with continuing current law. More recent CBO projections have reduced the savings estimate to between $2.96 billion and $2.38 billion over ten years, because recent lower CRP enrollment eliminates some of the previously estimated savings.[9]

While many view a reduction in CRP acres as inevitable in the current fiscal climate, conservation and wildlife groups caution that too large a reduction could have adverse environmental and ecological impacts.[10] These groups point to the release of more than 20% of the current program acres as potentially causing a reduction in critical species habitat and an increase in soil erosion and decrease in water quality caused by planting highly erodible and marginal land.[11] Livestock and grain producers, on the other hand, generally support some reduction in CRP acres, citing high commodity and feed prices as a reason for additional land needed to expand feed grain production.[12] Other groups cite advances in technology and sustainable production practices in the last 10 to 15 years as a reason for reduced CRP acres.[13]

Table 2. Top Five Conservation Practices Installed on CRP Acres (Current as of February 2013)

Practice Code	Practice Description	Acres Enrolled	Leading States
CP2	Establishment of permanent native grasses	7,177,546	Texas, Colorado, Kansas
CP10	Already established vegetative cover (grasses and legumes)	5,184,696	Texas, Montana, Colorado
CP1	Establishment of permanent introduced grasses and legumes	3,244,354	Missouri, Montana, Texas
CP4D	Permanent wildlife habitat	2,302,507	Colorado, North Dakota, Kansas
CP25	Rare and declining habitat	1,755,463	Kansas, Nebraska, Montana

Source: USDA, FSA, Conservation Practices Installed on CRP (acres), *Cumulative*, February 2013.

Note: Based on total acres enrolled in practices for all sign-up types.

Some forecast that the current high commodity price level will continue for the foreseeable future, thus possibly shrinking farmer interest in CRP for some time (see "Enrollment" discussion below).[14] Also, increased commodity prices can lead to increased land rental rates, which in turn increases the cost of land retirement programs such as CRP. These factors could signal a shift in farm bill conservation policy away from the traditional land retirement programs toward an increased focus on conservation working lands programs—which keep land in production while implementing conservation practices that address natural resource concerns—e.g., the Environmental Quality Incentives Program (EQIP) or the Conservation Stewardship Program (CSP).

Harvesting and Grazing

Harvesting and grazing is permitted on CRP land under certain conditions. Managed harvesting (including harvesting biomass) is permitted one out of every three years if approved in advanced and conducted according to a vegetative management plan. Routine grazing is permitted for the control of invasive species, also if approved in advanced and conducted according to a vegetative management plan and schedule. In limited situations, harvesting and grazing may be conducted in response to drought or other emergency. All harvesting and grazing, including in the event of an emergency, is prohibited during primary nesting season for birds. All activities also require a payment reduction commensurate with the economic value of the authorized activity.[15] Historically, this reduction ranges between 10%-25% of the annual rental payment. In many cases environmentally sensitive land is ineligible for harvesting and grazing.

During the summer of 2012, USDA announced a new process for responding to natural disasters, including emergency harvesting and grazing under CRP.[16] USDA lowered the payment reduction rate for emergency harvesting and grazing from 25% to 10%. In August 2012, USDA announced an additional 3.8 million CRP acres could be eligible to harvest and graze.[17] Many of these acres had previously been ineligible due to wetland characteristics and sensitive specialty practices (see the programmatic environmental assessment discussion in the text box below). As of February 12, 2013, 53 counties, all located in Texas, have been approved for emergency grazing under CRP.[18]

CRP AND THE NATIONAL ENVIRONMENTAL POLICY ACT (NEPA)

In May 2008, USDA announced that 24 million acres of CRP land could be applied in 2008 to a critical feed use (CFU) initiative. The initiative allowed CRP participants with established vegetative cover to voluntarily modify their CRP contracts to use certain CRP lands for managed harvesting and grazing without a payment reduction. The National Wildlife Federation (NWF) and NWF chapters in six states sought an injunction against USDA for failure to conduct an appropriate environmental review of the proposed CFU initiative. In June 2008, the U.S. District Court for the Western District of Washington agreed with NWF and issued a temporary restraining order (TRO). By July 2008, the court issued a permanent injunction, suspending the CFU initiative except for those who had been approved by or had applied to FSA prior to the TRO, or who had invested at least $4,500 toward harvesting or grazing equipment and preparation prior to the TRO.[19]

Following the passage of the 2008 farm bill, FSA issued a final supplemental environmental impact statement (SEIS) in June 2010.[20] In large part, the SEIS only evaluated the potential environmental impacts resulting from changes made by the 2008 farm bill. CRP harvesting and grazing activities were conducted in accordance with the 2010 SEIS until 2012, when USDA announced a modified use of emergency harvesting and grazing on CRP land. Because the 2012 emergency harvesting and grazing announcement authorized certain practices that were ineligible under the 2010 SEIP, FSA issued a final Programmatic Environmental Assessment (PEA) in August 2012.[21] The PEA included a mitigated finding of no significant impact (FONSI). FSA determined that certain mitigation measures were required to ensure that there are no significant environmental impacts, including: implementing a modified conservation plan, leaving 25% of the field ungrazed or no more than 75% of the approved stocking rate may be used, leaving 50% of each field unharvested, not harvesting or grazing the same acreage more than once, and limiting harvesting to one cutting.

The 2012 drought has fueled questions about the potential reduction of CRP acres (see "Farm Bill Expiration, Extension, and Reauthorization" above). It is unclear what level of relief to livestock is achieved through the emergency harvesting and grazing during drought or if there is any long-term impact on wildlife habitat. Other questions remain, including, if fewer acres were enrolled in CRP for conserving uses, or if enrollment were limited to more sensitive land that would not support harvesting and grazing, what impact would this have on livestock when drought strikes again? Is the role of CRP to provide drought relief or is that beyond the scope of the program? What level of payment reduction, if any, should be required for emergency harvesting and grazing? What are the positive and negative effects of harvesting and grazing, whether managed or in the event of emergency, that might impact wildlife, plant quality, and erosion control?

Enrollment

The nature of CRP enrollment has changed since the program's inception in the 1985 farm bill. Program priorities have shifted, total acres enrolled has fluctuated (see Figure 1 and Figure 2), farming technologies have advanced, and producer preferences have changed. Many of these changes are cited as a reason to further alter the level of CRP acres enrolled in the future.

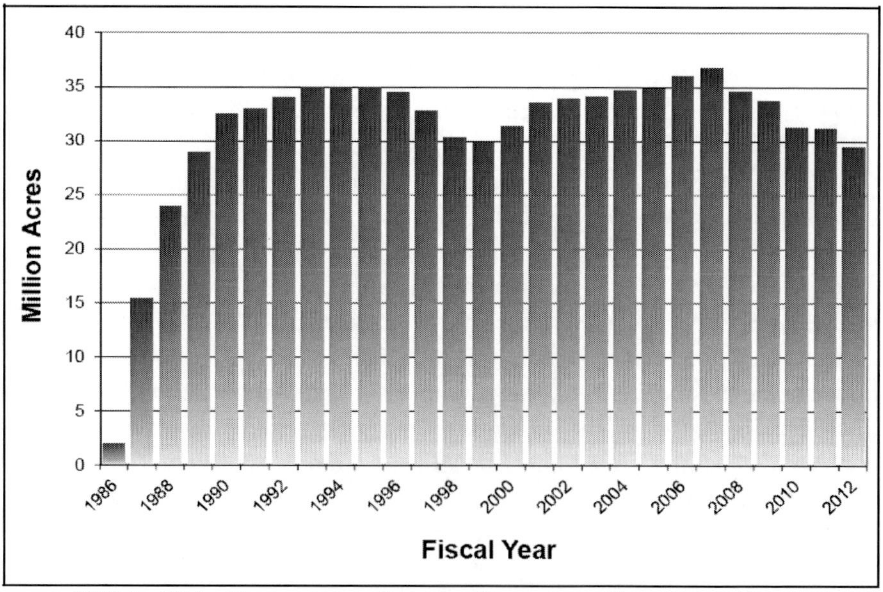

Source: USDA, FSA, *Conservation Reserve Program— Cumulative Enrollment by Year (Acres)*, http://www.fsa.usda.gov/Internet/FSA_File/ historystate8612.xls.

Figure 1. Cumulative CRP Enrollment (acres by fiscal year).

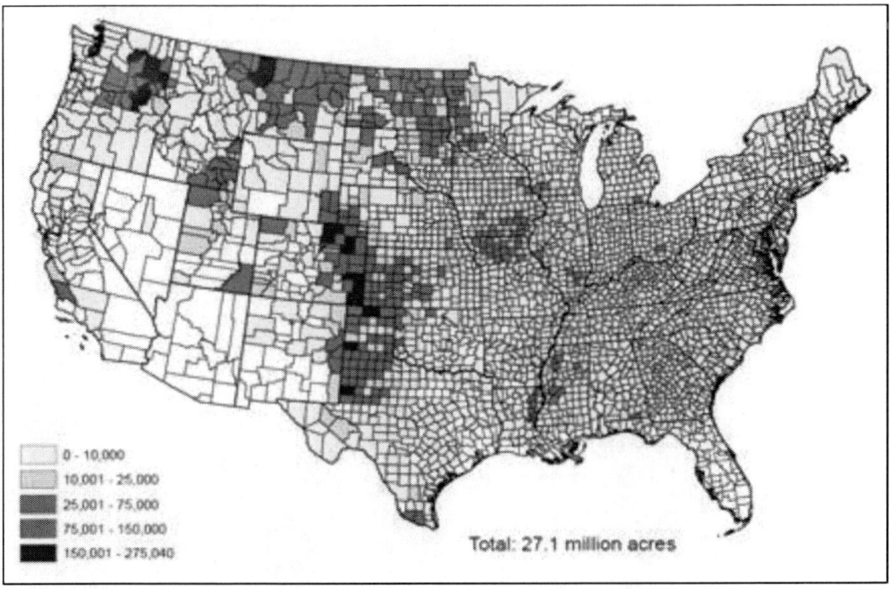

Source: USDA, FSA/EPAS/NRA, *CRP Enrollment— December 2012*, http://www.fsa.usda.gov/Internet/ FSA_File/crpenroll1212.pdf.

Figure 2. CRP Enrollment (acres enrolled as of December 2012).

Expiration of Contracts

CRP contracts vary in length, though most are 10 years in duration. At the end of a contract, the participant may seek either reenrollment into the program (via a general or continuous sign-up, if eligible) or let the contract expire. This 10-year cycle resulted in more than 16 million acres enrolled in 1997 potentially expiring all at once in 2007. To stagger this expiration process, USDA offered two- to five-year reenrollment and extension contracts in 2006 to contacts expiring between 2007 and 2010 (27 million acres). While approximately 83% of those offered accepted these extensions (23 million acres), over 8.5 million acres expired from the program during that time.

The 43rd general sign-up in 2012 accepted 3.8 million acres of new and reenrollment offers into CRP. Prior to this reenrollment opportunity, approximately 6.5 million acres under CRP contract (both general and continuous) were scheduled to expire on September 30, 2012.[22] This was considered to be a relatively large number of acres to potentially expire in one year, given that it will be three years before another 6 million additional acres under contract are scheduled to expire.[23] Ultimately, 3.2 million acres left CRP in FY2013, either through contract expiration or attrition. Between FY2007 and through FY2013, over 15.1 million CRP acres under contact have expired and were not reenrolled in the program (Figure 3). The majority of these acres in FY2013 are located in the central part of the United States, which also has the largest number of acres enrolled (Figure 4 and Figure 2). The number and location of these acres concerns some program advocates because of the potential loss of environmental benefits, particularly migratory and grassland bird habitat.

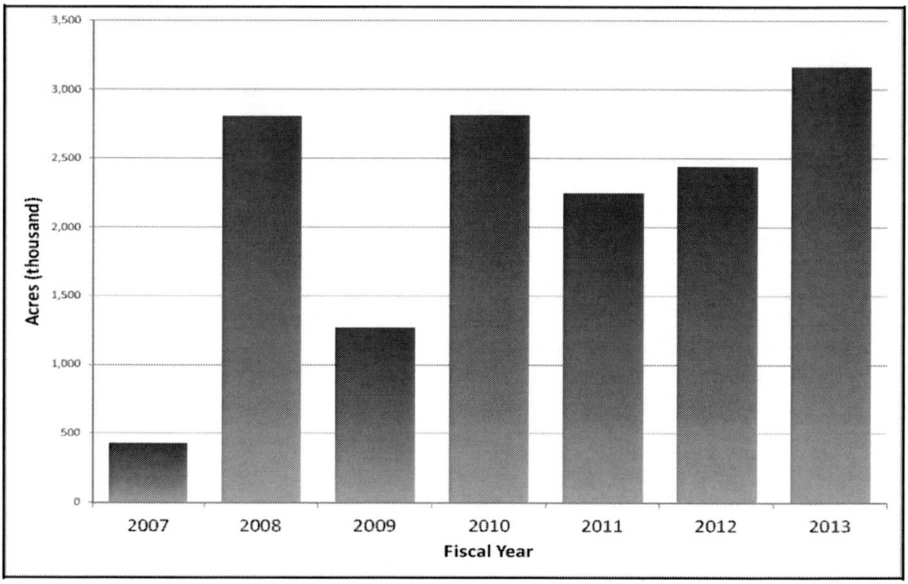

Source: USDA, FSA, *Changes in CRP Acreage from 2007 to October 2013 2013 by State,* http://www.fsa.usda.gov/ Internet/FSA_File/acresstate012213.xls.

Notes: Annual sum of expiring land that was not reenrolled and land lost through attrition. FY2013 land may be cropped in the 2013 crop year.

Figure 3. CRP Acres Not Reenrolled and Lost through Attrition, FY2007-FY2013.

Reenrollment of Acreage

Under the 1985 farm bill, CRP was initially authorized to enroll up to 45 million acres between crop years 1986 and 1990. USDA did not reach this enrollment cap and subsequent farm bills reduced the authorized level of enrollment.[24] CRP enrollment reached its peak in 2007 with 36.8 million acres. The 2008 farm bill reduced the enrollment cap to 32 million acres, thus reducing the opportunity for reenrollment of expiring acres under contact. Of the 6.5 million acres in CRP that could have expired at the end of FY2012, the most recent general sign-up (#43) reenrolled 3.3 million acres and 560,000 new acres.[25] Without a reauthorization of the program and funding authority, the program will no longer be able to enroll any new acres or reenroll acres as contracts expire.

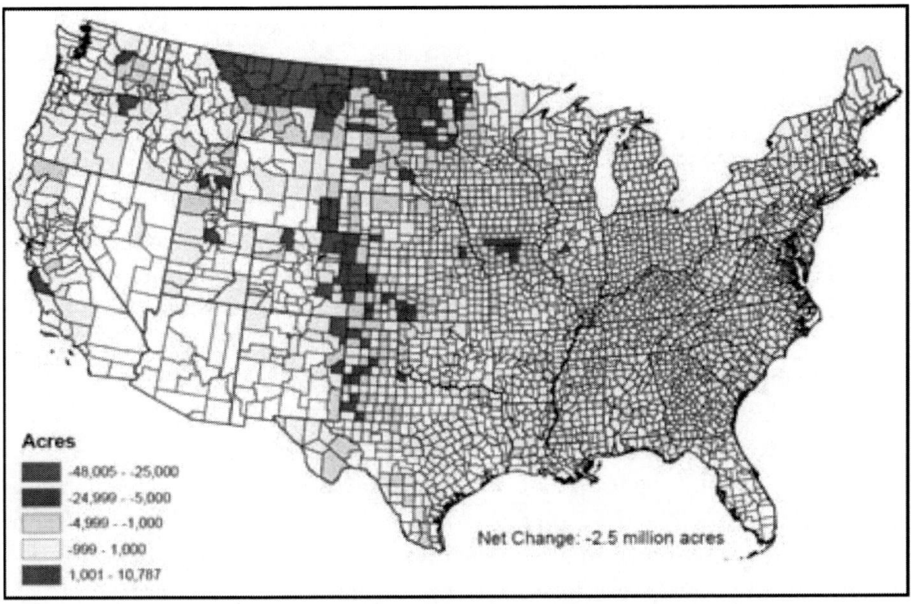

Source: USDA, FSA, EPA, NRA, *CRP Change in Enrollment from September to October 2012,* http://www.fsa.usda.gov/Internet/FSA_File/acresmapseptoct 2012.pdf.

Notes: Contracts expire September 30; most new contracts begin October 1.

Figure 4. Change in CRP Enrollment between September and October 2012.

Sixty-one percent of 2012 acres expiring under CRP contract were offered for reenrollment in sign-up #43. While this is below the 83% reenrollment rate under the 2006-2010 effort, it is consistent with other general sign-ups.[26] Other factors, such as higher commodity and land prices, may explain the decline, as well as potential differences between CRP annual rental payments and local rental rates (see "Rental Rates" section).[27] Approximately 2 million acres will expire in FY2014 and therefore may be offered for reenrollment in sign-up #45.

Contract Termination and Early Release

Under current law, a producer wishing to terminate a CRP contract early faces a penalty of full repayment, with interest, of all the funds already paid to the producer, including any cost-share payments and other financial incentives, plus a fee of 25% of rental payments received.

As demand for farmland increases, so does the pressure for USDA to "release" or terminate CRP contracts early and possibly waive any penalty. This has been particularly true since 2008 when corn prices hit record highs and have remained high.[28] A number of commodity organizations and livestock associations have been vocal about seeking release of CRP land from its contracts in order to expand crop production.[29] Conversely, others have pointed out that CRP is a voluntary program, in which land is competitively enrolled. Participants accepted federal funds in exchange for retiring land from production and converting it to conserving uses. If acres were allowed to return to production without penalty some question whether this violates the purpose of the program and diminishes the program's environmental gains.[30]

Although the Secretary of Agriculture always has the authority to release land from CRP without penalty, this option has not been commonly used. In program history, this option has been exercised twice—in 1995 and 1996—when acres were allowed a voluntary, penalty-free early release in order to enroll more environmentally sensitive cropland. In both cases, environmentally sensitive acres were not released and certain restrictions applied to acres returning to production or harvesting and grazing.

Rental Rates

CRP rental payments are based on two main factors: the county average rental rate and soil productivity. The county average rental rate uses the National Agricultural Statistics Service's (NASS) survey of county average rental rates for cropland and pastureland. Soil productivity is based on a Natural Resources Conservation Service (NRCS) calculation that uses data of the local soil, landscape, and climate to determine the ability of the land to produce crops on non-irrigated soil. The average CRP rental payment rates are as follows: $49.95 per acre for general sign-up, $93.05 per acre for non-CREP continuous sign-up, $133.56 per acre for CREP continuous sign-up, and $109.92 per acre for farmable wetlands.[31]

Rental rates for CRP contracts became an important issue to some producers when commodity prices began to rise in 2008. Commodity prices have remained high, causing producers to claim that CRP rental rates are significantly lower than the producers could get by renting their land out for production. On the other hand, contracts are for ten or more years and could be viewed as long-term investments rather than reactions to short-term commodity price fluctuation.

Economic Research Service Study

If rental rates are set too low, producers might decline to enroll their land, or, if already enrolled, they might decline to renew their contracts at expiration. A 2011 study by the Economic Research Service (ERS) at USDA, modeled the effect of increasing commodity prices on CRP enrollment.[32] The study suggested that maintaining CRP under its current configuration could lead to program cost increases. When constraints were placed on increasing rental rates, the study suggested that enrollment goals could be met with moderate increases in the CRP rental rates. The latter scenario might mean that enrollment goals could be met, but at the cost of applying a lower EBI, as producers with profitable, but environmentally sensitive, acreage choose not to enroll.

If crop prices remain high and enrolling environmentally sensitive land continues to be a program priority, then finding the level of rental payments that encourages enrollment and keeps the cost of the program acceptable to policy makers might continue to be an issue.

Office of the Inspector General Report

In July 2012, the USDA Office of Inspector General (OIG) issued a report on the use of CRP rental rates.[33] The report concluded that for the 39th general sign-up in 2010, FSA(1) did not use the most recent NRCS soil productivity factors; and (2) allowed states and counties to propose alternate rates that did not adhere to its own policies for reviewing and approving the alternate rates.[34] OIG accepted two of the four agency responses to its recommendations. The two responses that it found unacceptable concerned the use of the most recent NRCS productivity data and establishing procedures for approving alternate county average rental rates. It is unclear what follow-up action, if any, will be taken by FSA to address the remaining concerns.

Increases in Enrollment

Despite the potential limiting factors affecting CRP enrollment, the number of acres enrolled under continuous sign-ups, including for the Conservation Reserve Enhancement Program (CREP, see **Appendix**), has increased. Continuous sign-ups allow landowners to enroll land in certain high priority practices in exchange for additional financial incentive. As of

February 2013, almost 5.4 million acres (20%) are enrolled through continuous sign-up, an increase of 1.8 million acres since 2007. The additional financial incentive under continuous sign-up could offset the potential gap between CRP rental payments and local rental rates to enroll more environmentally sensitive acres. Currently, more contracts and farms are enrolled under continuous sign-ups (409,573 and 238,565, respectively) than for general sign-ups (291,395 and 195,061, respectively).[35] Continuous sign-up enrollment represents a fraction of the total CRP acreage because, in general, these enrollments involve only a small portion of a farmer's total acreage.

Environmental Benefits

The greatest concern over a reduced level of CRP acres is a reduced level of environmental benefits. Since its inception, research has shown that CRP has contributed to reduced levels of soil erosion, water quality improvement, and wildlife habitat development. While these benefits vary across the country, some conclude that without CRP there could be additional environmental degradation from agricultural production.[36] Table 3 includes a list of conservation practices applied on CRP land that is set to expire from the program between FY2014 and FY2017. It is unknown how many of the practices would expire as a result of acres not reenrolling in CRP due to the reduced number of authorized acres. It is also unknown whether these practices would be maintained without a CRP contract. Landowners may choose to continue these practices voluntarily or through other federal, state, or local assistance. In large part, the majority of practices that could be lost if allowed to expire would be grasslands, both native and introduced species, new and existing plantings.

According to FSA, since 2002, CRP has reduced soil erosion by 325 million tons from pre-CRP levels each year. Since the program's inception in 1986, CRP has reduced more than 8 billion tons of soil erosion. Through FY2010, CRP has enrolled more than 2 million acres in wetlands and over 2 million in buffers. Other annual conservation benefits include an equivalent of approximately 52 million metric ton net reduction in carbon dioxide (CO_2) from sequestration, reduced fuel use and nitrous oxide emissions avoided from no fertilizer use; more than 2 million acres of wildlife habitat established; and a reduction of about 607 million pounds of nitrogen and 122 million pounds of phosphorus.[37] From a wildlife perspective, it is estimated that CRP land produces over 13.5 million pheasants and 2.2 million ducks each year through habitat availability.[38]

CONCLUSION

As Congress considers reauthorization of the program as part of the farm bill, CRP, as the most expensive conservation program, could see a possible reduction of authorized acres to achieve a cost savings. Other pressures from high crop prices, increased demand for land, and the potentially low rental rates could also impact the program's ability to enroll the most desirable acres in the future. Despite these challenges supporters encourage maintaining CRP enrollment because of the numerous environmental gains achieved by the program, including improved water quality, soil health, and wildlife species habitat. Balancing the cost of maintaining such benefits with the cost of the program could continue to be a challenge for Congress.

Table 3. Top Ten Expiring CRP Conservation Practices (by expiring year in total acres applied)

Practice Code	Practice Description	2014	2015	2016	2017
Total Expiring Acres		1,992,756	1,674,088	1,195,403	2,647,137
CP01	Introduced grasses and legume	140,314	135,100	106,925	188,275
CP02	Native grasses	584,006	488,526	316,164	283,793
CP03H	Hardwood trees	77,873	59,385	5,388	31,800
CP04D	Permanent wildlife habitat	218,588	127,960	120,415	119,064
CP10	Existing grasses and legumes	222,604	164,116	81,697	1,353,896
CP11	Existing trees	17,853	39,479	36,817	112,723
CP21	Filter strips-grass	79,627	108,748	114,998	95,129
CP22	Riparian buffers	52,769	113,686	137,180	110,529
CP23	Wetland restoration	278,146	96,512	26,808	29,702
CP25	Rare and declining habitat	145,356	130,978	58,277	17,944

Source: CRS, developed from USDA, FSA data, April 2012.

APPENDIX. CONTINUOUS SIGN-UP INITIATIVES

Continuous sign-up is designed to enroll the most environmentally sensitive land into CRP through specific conservation practices or resource needs. Continuous sign-up includes a number of initiatives that target acres with specific resource concerns or support additional conservation practices. These are described below.

Conservation Reserve Enhancement Program (CREP)

Initially implemented in 1997, CREP is a joint federal-state continuous sign-up program under CRP. CREP targets geographic regions with agricultural-related environmental concerns, such as Maryland's Chesapeake Bay and Florida's Everglades. Some states (e.g., New York and Ohio) have multiple CREP projects, each targeting a different area of the state. Projects are designed to address specific environmental objectives through targeted CRP enrollments. Sign-ups are continuous, non-competitive, and typically provide additional financial incentives beyond annual rental payments and cost-share assistance. There are currently 45 CREP agreements in 33 states.

Farmable Wetlands Program (FWP)

The Farmable Wetlands Program (FWP) enrolls farmable or prior converted wetlands into CRP. In exchange for additional financial incentives, landowners agree to restore the hydrology of the wetland, establish vegetative cover, and prohibit development. For land to be considered eligible it must meet one of the following criteria:

- a wetland or converted wetland cropped at least 3 of the immediately preceding 10 crop years;
- a constructed wetland that receives flow from a row crop agriculture drainage system and is designed to provide nitrogen removal in addition to other wetland functions;
- land in a commercial pond-raised aquaculture in any year between 2002 through 2007; or

- cropland that was cropped at least three of ten crop years between 1990 and 2002, and is subject to the natural overflow of a prairie wetland.

The enrollment of buffer acreage is also permitted to enhance wildlife benefits. No more than 100,000 acres may be enrolled in FWP in any state[39] and no more than 1 million acres nationally. The enrollment of wetlands (described under the first and second bullets above) is limited to 40 contiguous acres. "Flooded farmland," or that defined in the fourth bullet above, is limited to 20 contiguous acres, and has a 20-acre limit.

Emergency Forestry CRP

Following the 2005 hurricane season, Congress created the Emergency Forestry Conservation Reserve Program (EFCRP) in the Emergency Supplemental Appropriations Act of 2006 (P.L. 109-148). The program provides assistance to nonindustrial private forest land damaged by the 2005 hurricanes (specifically Katrina and Rita) in Gulf Coast states. Over $504 million in mandatory funding was authorized to carry out this program. Acreage enrolled in this program does not count toward the total CRP enrollment cap. As of December 31, 2011, a total of 294,318 acres had been enrolled in Alabama, Florida, Louisiana, Mississippi, and Texas, with payments totaling over $85.8 million.

Transition Incentive Program (TIP)

The 2008 farm bill authorized a new option for expiring CRP contracts. Under the Transition Incentive Program (TIP), land from expiring CRP contracts may be transitioned back into sustainable grazing or crop production by a beginning or socially disadvantaged farmer or rancher. The land must be from a retired or retiring owner or operator (not a family member) in exchange for up to two additional years of annual CRP rental payments following the expiration of the CRP contract. The program was authorized to spend up to $25 million between FY2009 and FY2012.

Table A-1. CRP Initiatives

Initiative	Year Started	Allocation (acres)	Current Enrollment (acres)[a]
Floodplain Wetlands	2004	600,000	232,098
Bottomland Hardwood Trees	2004	250,000	84,709
Non-floodplain and Playa Wetlands	2005	350,000	226,806
Upland Bird Habitat Buffers	2005	500,000	242,087
Longleaf Pine Plantings	2007	250,000	117,060
Duck Nesting Habitat	2007	300,000	194,485
State Acres for Wildlife Enhancement (SAFE)	2008	1,250,000	699,305
Highly Erodible Land	2012	750,000	43,737
Pollinator Habitat	2012	100,000	[b]

Source: USDA, FSA, *Conservation Reserve Program*, Monthly Summary, August 2012, http://www.fsa.usda.gov/ Internet/FSA_File/crpstataug2012.pdf.

a. Cumulative acres as of February 2013. Excludes lands enrolled in CREPs.

b. To date, sign-up results for this initiative are not available.

Other Initiatives

Several other initiatives under CRP have been developed over time, mostly in response to Administration priorities. Table A-1 includes a list of recent initiatives and their enrollment size.

End Notes

[1] USDA, FSA, *Conservation Reserve Program Sign-Up 45 Environmental Benefits Index (EBI)*, Fact Sheet, February 2013, http://www.fsa.usda.gov/Internet/FSA_File/su45ebi factsheet.pdf.

[2] USDA, FSA, *Conservation Reserve Program*, Monthly Summary, February 2013, http:// www.fsa.usda.gov/Internet/ FSA_File/feb2013summary.pdf.

[3] Both CREP and the farmable wetlands programs are discussed in the **Appendix**.

[4] 7 C.F.R. 1410.5. Producers must also meet broader eligibility requirements related to adjusted gross income limits (not more than $1 million) and compliance requirements.

[5] 16 U.S.C. 3831(b).

[6] Refers to a conservation plan developed under the highly erodible land conservation provisions. For additional information, see CRS Report R42459, *Conservation Compliance and U.S. Farm Policy*, by Megan Stubbs.

[7] 32 million acres under the 2008 farm bill authorization, 16 U.S.C. 3831(d).

[8] For example, the highest average rental payment per acre for a state (for all CRP sign-ups) is in Massachusetts at $207.20/acre. Only 10 acres are enrolled in Massachusetts. The lowest average rental payment for a state is in Wyoming at $26.46/acre. The state with the most acres enrolled—Texas with 3.3 million acres—averages $37.19/acre for rental payments.

[9] Letter from Douglas W. Elmendorf, Director, to Honorable Debbie Stabenow, Chairwoman of the Committee on Agriculture, Nutrition, and Forestry, March 1, 2013.

[10] Sara Hooper, Environmental Defense Fund, *Statement for the Record*, Testimony before the U.S. House of Representatives Committee on Agriculture Subcommittee on Conservation, Energy, and Forestry, Concerning Formulation of the 2012 Farm Bill: Conservation Programs, April 26, 2012, http://agriculture.house.gov/sites/ republicans.agriculture.house. gov/files/pdf/hearings/Hopper120426.pdf.

[11] Josephine Marcotty, "Open Land Falling to the Plow," *StarTribune*, August 6, 2012.

[12] Chris Clayton, "NGFA Wants to Take a Bite Out of CRP," *DTN Progressive Farmer*, April 4, 2012.

[13] Bruce Knight, *ReGaining Ground: A Conservation Reserve Program Right-Sized for the Times*, Strategic Conservation Solutions for National Grain and Feed Foundation, June 2012, http://www.ngfa.org/files/ SCSReGainingGroundResearchStudyforNGFF%286-8-2012%29.pdf.

[14] Daniel Hellerstein and Scott Malcolm, *The Influence of Raising Commodity Prices on the Conservation Reserve Program,* USDA, ERS, ERR-110, Washington, DC, February, 2011, http://www.ers.usda.gov/Publications/ERR110/ERR110.pdf.

[15] 16 U.S.C. 3832(d).

[16] USDA, FSA, "USDA Announces Streamlined Disaster Designation Process with Lower Emergency Loan Rates and Greater CRP Flexibility in Disaster Areas," press release, July 11, 2012, http://www.fsa.usda.gov/FSA/printapp? fileName=nr_20120711_rel_0228.html& newsType=newsrel.

[17] USDA, FSA, "Agriculture Secretary Vilsack Announces New Drought Assistance, Designates an Additional 218 Counties as Primary Natural Disaster Areas," press release, August 1, 2012, http://www.fsa.usda.gov/FSA/printapp?fileName=nr_20120801_rel_0260.html& newsType=newsrel.

[18] USDA, FSA, "Table—Drought and Counties Approved for Emergency Haying and Grazing," February 12, 2013, http://www.fsa.usda.gov/Internet/FSA_File/haylist021213.xls.

[19] *National Wildlife Federation v. Ed Schaefer, USDA*, CV08-1004-JCC (U.S. District Court Western District of Washington at Seattle 2008).

[20] USDA, FSA, *Conservation Reserve Program—Supplemental Environmental Impact Statement*, Final, June 2010, http://www.fsa.usda.gov/Internet/FSA_File/crpfinalseismaster61010.pdf.

[21] USDA, FSA, *Programmatic Environmental Assessment*, Emergency Drought Response on Conservation Reserve Program Lands, August 2012, http://www.fsa.usda.gov/Internet/ FSA_File/haygraz_pea_fonziv2_0812.pdf.

[22] CRP closed the 2012 fiscal year with approximately 27 million acres enrolled. The maximum enrollment level prior to the September 30, 2012, expiration was 32 million acres.

[23] Including 3.3 million in FY2013, 2.0 million in FY2014, and 1.7 million in FY2015.

[24] The 1996 farm bill (P.L. 104-127) lowered the enrollment cap to a total of 36.4 million acres through CY2002. The 2002 farm bill (P.L. 107-171) increased the enrollment cap total to 39.2 million acres through CY2007.

[25] USDA, FSA, *The Conservation Reserve Program: 43rd Signup Results*, Washington, DC, June 12, 2012, Table 2, http://www.fsa.usda.gov/Internet/FSA_File/su43state072512.pdf.

[26] Personal communication with FSA staff, June 1, 2012.

[27] Daniel Hellerstein, *Recent Conservation Reserve Program Enrollments Signal Changing Priorities*, USDA, ERS, Amber Waves, March 2012.

[28] Beginning in 2007, agricultural commodity prices rose significantly. These prices remain high today and according to USDA's long-term agricultural projection are expected to continue for corn, oilseeds, and many other crops at historically high levels. See, USDA, Office of

the Chief Economist, *USDA Agricultural Projections to 2022*, OCE-2013-1, Washington, DC, February 2013, http://www.ers.usda.gov/media/1013566/oce131fm.pdf.

[29] While many requested a CRP "early-out" option in 2008, the Bush Administration took no action regarding this option. See May 27, 2008, press call with Secretary Schafer, http://www.usda.gov/wps/portal/usda/usdahome?contentidonly=true&contentid=2008/05/0138.xml. Instead, the Administration allowed for expanded harvesting and grazing, which resulted in a lawsuit (see text box above). The pressure for early contract termination continues; for example, in 2011, Representative Nunes, along with 25 other Members of Congress, signed a letter asking the President to release CRP land without penalty for the purpose of grain production. Letter from Devin Nunes, Representative, to Barack Obama, President, April 8, 2011. The Obama Administration did not allow CRP contract terminations without penalty.

[30] Allison Winter, "USDA conservation program imperiled by soaring crop prices, floods," *Greenwire*, June 26, 2008.

[31] USDA, FSA, *Conservation Reserve Program - Monthly Summary*, Washington, DC, February 2013.

[32] Daniel Hellerstein and Scott Malcolm, *The Influence of Rising Commodity Prices on the Conservation Reserve Program*, USDA, ERS, Economic Research Report number 110, February 2011.

[33] USDA, OIG, *Farm Service Agency, Conservation Reserve Program - Soil Rental Rates*, Audit Report 03601-0051-Te, July 2012.

[34] For example, "of the 687 proposed alternate rates it received, FSA's national office approved 686, even though it determined the majority (669 of 687) of the proposals contained evidence to support the alternate rates to be less than strong." Under the 41st general sign-up, a total of 271 proposals were submitted for alternate county average rental rates. According to OIG, one official approved 150 rates—105 exceeded the NASS rate and 45 were lower than the NASS rate. Ibid.

[35] USDA, FSA, *Conservation Reserve Program*, Monthly Summary, July 2012, http://www.fsa.usda.gov/Internet/ FSA_File/july2012crpstat.pdf.

[36] JunJie Wu and Bruce Weber, *Implications of a Reduced Conservation Reserve Program*, The Council on Food, Agriculture & Resource Economics, July 2012.

[37] USDA, FSA, *The Environmental Benefits of the Conservation Reserve Program*, United States —2010, July 2011, http://www.fsa.usda.gov/Internet/FSA_File/united_states.pdf.

[38] National Wildlife Federation, *Maintaining Benefits of Expiring CRP*, http://www.nwf.org/Wildlife/Policy/Farm-Bill/ Farm-Bill-Success-Stories/Success-Expiring-CRP.aspx.

[39] This limit may be increased by USDA to up to 200,000 acres per state.

In: Conservation Provisions ...
Editor: Arianna R. Hills
ISBN: 978-1-61122-559-4

Chapter 3

CONSERVATION COMPLIANCE AND U.S. FARM POLICY*

Megan Stubbs

SUMMARY

The Food Security Act of 1985 (P.L. 99-198, 1985 farm bill) included a number of significant conservation provisions designed to reduce production and conserve soil and water resources. Many of the provisions remain in effect today, including the two compliance provisions—highly erodible land conservation (sodbuster) and wetland conservation (swampbuster). The two provisions, collectively referred to as conservation compliance, require that in exchange for certain U.S. Department of Agriculture (USDA) program benefits, a producer agrees to maintain a minimum level of conservation on highly erodible land and not to convert wetlands to crop production.

Conservation compliance affects most USDA benefits administered by the Farm Service Agency (FSA) and the Natural Resources Conservation Service (NRCS). These benefits can include commodity support payments, disaster payments, farm loans, and conservation program payments, to name a few. If a producer is found to be in violation of conservation compliance, then a number of penalties could be enforced. These penalties range from temporary

* This is an edited, reformatted and augmented version of a Congressional Research Service publication R42459, prepared for Members and Committees of Congress dated November 4, 2013.

exemptions that allow the producer time to correct the violation, to a determination that the producer is ineligible for any USDA farm payment and must pay back current and prior years' benefits.

As Congress considers the reauthorization of farm policy in the next farm bill, issues related to conservation compliance have emerged. The reduction in soil erosion from highly erodible land conservation continues, but at a slower pace than following enactment of the 1985 farm bill. The leveling off of erosion reductions leaves broad policy questions related to conservation compliance, including whether an acceptable level of soil erosion on cropland has been achieved; whether additional reductions could be achieved, and if so, at what cost; and how federal farm policy should encourage additional reductions in erosion. These broad policy questions, in addition to general concerns of program oversight and implementation, continue to influence the farm bill debate.

One of the most controversial farm bill proposals involves adding crop insurance subsidies to the list of benefits that could be lost if a producer is found to be out of compliance. Federal crop insurance subsidies were originally included as a benefit that could be denied under the compliance provisions. However, they were removed in the 1996 farm bill to increase producer flexibility, while at the same time direct payments were added. Presently, high commodity prices have resulted in few or no counter-cyclical payments, leaving conservation program participation and direct payments as the remaining major benefits that might motivate producer compliance with conservation requirements. The Senate-passed farm bill (S. 954) would eliminate countercyclical and direct payments, and re-tie federal crop insurance subsidies to compliance requirements. The House-passed farm bill (H.R. 2642) would also eliminate direct payments, but does not tie crop insurance subsidies to compliance requirements. Re-tying crop insurance subsidies to compliance requirements has been met with mixed reviews. Most in the conservation and environmental community support the requirement, while some producer groups and the crop insurance industry are wary of the linkage. Separately, the Senate and House bills establish a "sodsaver" provision for new crop production on native sod. The provision reduces crop insurance premium subsidies and prohibits benefits under the Noninsured Crop Disaster or general commodity programs on land that has never been tilled. Conference negotiations to reconcile the two bills are ongoing.

Federal policies and programs traditionally have offered voluntary incentives to producers to plan and apply resource-conserving practices on private lands. It was not until the 1980s that Congress took an alternative approach to agricultural conservation through enactment of the Food Security Act of 1985 (P.L. 99-198, 1985 farm bill). The bill's more publicized provisions—the Conservation Reserve Program (CRP),[1] highly erodible land conservation (sodbuster), and wetland conservation (swampbuster)[2]—remain significant today. The latter two "conservation compliance" provisions require that in exchange for certain U.S. Department of Agriculture (USDA) program benefits, a producer agrees to maintain a minimum level of conservation on highly erodible land and not to convert wetlands to crop production. As Congress continues to debate the reauthorization of the farm bill, questions surrounding conservation compliance have arisen, such as how it works, whether it is effective, who it impacts, how it has changed over time, and how it might continue if current farm programs change. One of the most controversial issues has been whether conservation compliance should be tied to federal crop insurance subsidies.

RECENT DEVELOPMENTS

The Senate passed the Agriculture Reform, Food, and Jobs Act of 2013 (S. 954) on June 10, 2013, and the House passed the Federal Agriculture Reform and Risk Management Act of 2012 (H.R. 2642) on July 11, 2013. Conference negotiations on the two bills (H.R. 2642 and S. 954) formally began on October 30, 2013.[3]

Both bills eliminate select farm programs that are currently tied to conservation compliance—direct payments and counter-cyclical payments—while adding new farm programs (e.g., Agricultural Crop Risk, ARC) to the list of affected benefits. Similarities between the two bills exist; however, larger differences related to crop insurance benefits, the sodsaver provision, and wetland mitigation will require negotiation during conference.

Crop Insurance Linkage

In addition to other conservation changes, the Senate-passed bill re-ties federal crop insurance premium subsidies to conservation compliance requirements (discussed further below, in the "Issues for Congress" section).[4] To maintain eligibility for crop insurance premium subsidies, producers on highly erodible land would have approximately five years to develop and implement an approved conservation plan. The Senate-passed bill also grants producers time (one to two years) to mitigate wetland conservation (swampbuster) violations before becoming ineligible for crop insurance premium subsidies.

Unlike the Senate-passed bill, the House-passed bill does not re-tie crop insurance subsidies to conservation compliance requirements. An amendment to include language similar to the Senate bill was offered on the House floor during debate, but was withdrawn.[5]

Sodsaver

Both the House- and Senate-passed bills include a new "sodsaver" provision (described further in the "Conservation Compliance Today" section). Under both bills, crop insurance premium subsidies would be reduced by 50 percentage points for production on native sod during the first four years of planting.[6] Crops planted on native sod would also be ineligible for the Noninsured Crop Assistance Program (NAP) and general commodity support programs.

For new crop insurance policies, crop yield guarantees could also be affected. The yield guarantee for a crop insurance policy is a producer's "normal" crop yield based on actual production history. In the absence of actual yield data (e.g., production on native sod or no yield documentation on existing fields), a "transition yield" (T-yield) is assigned, which is based on a portion of 10-year average county yields for the crop. The House-passed bill would provide for a lower T-yield on native sod compared with other cropland when setting the initial yield guarantee on land with no available yield history.[7] The Senate-passed bill would provide the same T-yield for all cropland—general and native sod.[8]

When renewing crop insurance policies during the first four years of planting on native sod, both the House and Senate bills would prohibit producers from using potentially higher T-yields to replace potentially lower actual farm yields when establishing the annual yield guarantees for policies on individual farms.[9] "Yield substitution" is currently allowed on general cropland, which increases the yield guarantee and, if allowed, can increase the incentive to produce on native sod.

The House-passed version of sodsaver is limited to the Prairie Pothole National Priority Area (**Figure 1**), located in Montana, North Dakota, South Dakota, Minnesota, and Iowa, whereas the Senate-passed version would apply nationwide.

Wetlands Mitigation

Currently, landowners who wish to alter wetlands must mitigate or replace the lost functions in order to remain eligible for farm program benefits under Wetlands Conservation (see "Swampbuster" section, below). The House-passed bill would change the wetlands mitigation process, while the Senate-passed bill would require USDA to study the impacts of a potential change.

Current law states that mitigation should not require more than a 1-to-1 acreage substitution unless additional acreage is required to "provide equivalent functions and values" that would otherwise be lost as a result of the wetlands conversion to be mitigated.[10] The House-passed bill would remove the potential requirement of additional acreage and restrict wetland mitigation activities to not more than a 1-to-1 acreage basis.[11] The Senate bill requires USDA to review potential changes to the wetlands mitigation process and provide legislative recommendations no later than two years after the date of enactment.[12]

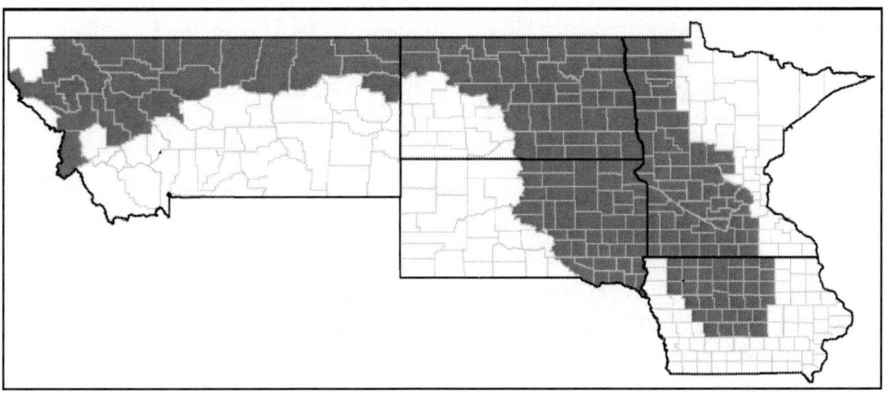

Source: USDA, RMA, Prairie Pothole National Priority Area, April 28, 2008, http://www.rma.usda.gov/data/pothole/2008/all_states.pdf.

Notes: States included in the Prairie Pothole National Priority Area (left to right) are Montana, North Dakota, South Dakota, Minnesota, and Iowa.

Figure 1. Prairie Pothole National Priority Area.

What Is "Highly Erodible"?

For land to be considered highly erodible (as defined under 16 U.S.C. 3801) it must be—

- land that currently has, or if put into agricultural production would have, an excessive average annual rate of erosion in relation to the soil loss tolerance level (see "The 'T'' Factor" text box, below); or
- cropland that is classified as class IV, VI, VII, or VIII land under the land capability classification system in effect on December 23, 1985.

The land capability classification system is an interpretive grouping on soil maps made primarily for agricultural purposes. Capability "classes" are broad categories of soils with similar hazards or limitations. There are eight classes, with soil damage and limitations on use becoming progressively greater from class I to class VIII.[13]

NRCS classifies about 101.1 million acres of U.S. cropland as highly erodible, approximately 27% of total cropland.

Conservation Compliance Today

The 1985 farm bill included a number of significant conservation provisions designed to reduce crop production and conserve soil and water resources. The highly erodible land conservation provision (sodbuster) introduced in the 1985 farm bill was not intended to "allow the Federal government to impose demands on any farmer or rancher concerning what may be done with their land; ... only that the Federal government will no longer subsidize producers who choose to convert highly erodible land to cropland unless they also agree to install conservation system(s) ... "[14] Similarly, the wetland conservation provision introduced in the 1985 farm bill does not authorize USDA "to regulate the use of private, or non-Federal land"; rather, "the objective of this provision is to deny various Federal benefits to those producers who choose to drain wetlands for the purpose of producing agricultural commodities."[15] Since the enactment of the 1985 farm bill, each succeeding farm bill has amended the compliance provisions. For a brief history of the farm bill legislative changes to the conservation compliance provisions since the 1985 farm bill, see Appendix A.

Sodbuster

The highly erodible land conservation provision, as enacted in the 1985 farm bill, introduced the concept that in exchange for certain federal farm benefits a producer must implement a minimum level of conservation. The provision, still in force today, applies the loss of benefits to land classified as highly erodible that was not in cultivation between 1980 and 1985 (i.e., newly broken land, referred to as sodbuster) and any highly erodible land in production after 1990, regardless of when the land was put into production. Land meeting this classification can be considered eligible for USDA program benefits if the land user agrees to cultivate the land using an approved conservation plan.

In addition to the application of an approved conservation plan, a number of exemptions are possible.[16]

- *Good faith.* If the person has acted in good faith and without the intent to violate the compliance provisions, then the producer may be granted up to one year to comply with a conservation plan.
- *Graduated penalty.* Under some circumstances, producers could be subject to a minimum of $500 and no more than $5,000 loss in benefits, rather than a loss of all benefits.
- *Allowable variance.* If a conservation system fails and the failure is determined to be technical and minor in nature, and to have little effect on the erosion control purposes of the conservation plan, then the producer may not be found out of compliance. Similarly, the producer may not be found out of compliance if the system failure was due to circumstances beyond the control of the producer.
- *Temporary variance.* A producer may be granted a temporary variance for practices prescribed in the conservation plan due to issues related to weather, pests, or disease. USDA has 30 days from the date of the request to issue a temporary variance determination; otherwise the variance is considered granted.
- *Economic hardship.* A local Farm Service Agency (FSA) county committee, with concurrence from the state or district FSA director and technical concurrence from the Natural Resources Conservation Service (NRCS), is allowed to permit relief if it is determined that a conservation system causes a producer undue economic hardship.

Swampbuster

The "swampbuster" or wetland conservation provision extends the sodbuster concept to wetland areas. Producers who plant a program crop on a wetland converted after December 23, 1985, or who convert wetlands, making agricultural commodity production possible, after November 28, 1990, are ineligible for certain USDA program benefits. This means that, for a producer to be found out of compliance, crop production does not actually have to occur; production only needs to be made possible through activities such as draining, dredging, filling, or leveling the wetland. Under the wetlands compliance provision, the following lands are considered exempt:

- a wetland converted to cropland before enactment (December 23, 1985);
- artificially created lakes, ponds, or wetlands;
- wetlands created by irrigation delivery systems;
- wetlands on which agricultural production is naturally possible;
- wetlands that are temporarily or incidentally created as a result of adjacent development activities;
- wetlands converted to cropland before December 23, 1985, that have reverted back to a wetland as the result of a lack of drainage, lack of management, or circumstances beyond the control of the landowner;
- wetlands converted if the effect of such action is minimal; and
- authorized wetlands converted through a permit issued under Section 404 of the Federal Water Pollution Control Act (33 U.S.C. 1344), for which wetland values, acreage, and functions of the converted wetland were adequately mitigated.

Sodsaver

The 2008 farm bill created a new compliance provision under the crop insurance title (Section 12020), known as sodsaver. The sodsaver provision makes producers who plant an insurable crop (5 or more acres) on native sod ineligible for crop insurance and the noninsured crop disaster assistance (NAP) program[17] for the first five years of planting. The conference agreement to the 2008 farm bill states that this provision may apply to virgin prairie converted to cropland in the Prairie Pothole National Priority Area (**Figure 1**), but only if elected by the state. USDA established a sign-up date of February 15, 2009, in which no governors opted to participate in the program. Additional opportunities to participate are possible, though thought unlikely, if the program remains voluntary.

Affected Program Benefits

As it exists today, conservation compliance applies to most farm program payments, loans, or other benefits administered by FSA and NRCS. Table 1 includes the statutory description and examples of specific USDA program benefits that are affected if a producer is found to be out of compliance with the highly erodible land and wetland conservation provisions. Conservation compliance provisions do not apply to the federal crop insurance program as administered by USDA's Risk Management Agency (RMA). If a producer requests any payment, loan, or other benefit subject to the conservation compliance provision, then the provision applies to all land owned by the producer or the producer's affiliates. This includes land located anywhere in the United States or U.S. territories, without regard to whether payments, loans, or other benefits are actually received for such land. In other words, if producers are found out of compliance on one portion of their land, they are deemed out of compliance for all land owned or associated with them, regardless of where it is located.

Implementation

Both NRCS and FSA implement conservation compliance as part of USDA farm programs. FSA has primary responsibility for making producer eligibility determinations about conservation compliance. NRCS has primary responsibility for technical determinations associated with conservation compliance. Each agency's role is outlined in Appendix B.

Following the 1985 farm bill, conservation compliance requirements created a large workload for NRCS staff. Compliance required that new plans be completed by 1990 on the approximately 140 million acres classified as highly erodible. In contrast, in 1984, the year before compliance was enacted, NRCS assisted with plans on about 2.5 million acres. Demands remained high ahead of the 1995 deadline for full implementation. Almost half of these plans were revised at least once before the 1995 deadline because of changes in farming techniques and crops, new conservation technology, and changes in ownership and tenancy.

Table 1. USDA Benefits Affected by Conservation Compliance

Statutory Description	Examples of Benefits
Contract payments under a production flexibility contract, marketing assistance loans, and any type of price support or payment made available under the Agricultural Market Transition Act, the Commodity Credit Corporation Charter Act (15 U.S.C. 714 et seq.), or any other Act.	Direct payments, counter-cyclical payments, Milk Income Loss Contract (MILC) payments, Average Crop Revenue Election (ACRE), and Marketing Assistance Loans
A farm storage facility loan made under Section 4(h) of the Commodity Credit Corporation Charter Act (15 U.S.C. 714b(h)).[a]	Farm Storage Facility Loan
Disaster payments[a]	Noninsured Crop Disaster Assistance program, ad hoc disaster assistance programs, Emergency Forest Restoration Program (EFRP), Emergency Assistance for Livestock, Honey Bees, and Farm-raised Fish (ELAP), Livestock Forage Program (LFP), Livestock Indemnity Program (LIP), Tree Assistance Program (TAP), and Supplemental Revenue Assurance (SURE)[b]
A farm credit program loan made, insured, or guaranteed under the Consolidated Farm and Rural Development Act or any other provision of law administered by FSA.[c]	FSA Farm Operating Loans, Farm Ownership Loans, and Emergency Disaster Loans
A payment made pursuant to a contract entered into under the Environmental Quality Incentives Program (EQIP) or any other provision of Subtitle D of the Food Security Act of 1985, as amended	Agricultural Water Enhancement Program (AWEP), Conservation Stewardship Program (CSP), Conservation Reserve Program (CRP), Environmental Quality Incentives Program (EQIP), Farmland Protection Program (FPP), Grassland Reserve Program

Statutory Description	Examples of Benefits
	(GRP), Wetlands Reserve Program (WRP), and Wildlife Habitat Incentives Program (WHIP).
A payment made under Section 401 or 402 of the Agricultural Credit Act of 1978 (16 U.S.C. 2201 or 2202).	Emergency Conservation Program (ECP) and Emergency Watershed Protection (EWP) Program
A payment, loan, or other assistance under Section 3 or 8 of the Watershed Protection and Flood Prevention Act (16 U.S.C. 1003 or 1006a).	Watershed Protection and Flood Prevention program

Source: 16 U.S.C. 3811 and 16 U.S.C. 3812.

Notes: The examples listed should not be considered an exhaustive list. Also affected would be any payments made under Section 4 or 5 of the Commodity Credit Corporation Charter Act (15 U.S.C. 714b or 714c) for the storage of an agricultural commodity acquired by the CCC.

a. Applies only to highly erodible land conservation provisions.

b. Authority expired September 30, 2011, for new contracts under EFRP, and for disaster payments under ELAP, LFP, LIP, TAP, and SURE for disasters occurring after that date.

c. Only applies if the proceeds of the loan will be used for a purpose that contributes to the conversion of wetlands that would make production of an agricultural commodity possible or for a purpose that contributes to excessive erosion of highly erodible land. Loans made before enactment of the 1985 farm bill are not affected.

Another dynamic of implementing compliance was the requirement for NRCS to work with a large number of new, and sometimes less cooperative, clients. Most producers receiving farm program benefits were familiar with FSA because the agency was already administering many federal farm programs. However, prior to 1985, conservation programs administered by NRCS were small and voluntary. Because conservation compliance tied federal farm program benefits to the requirement for a conservation plan, some producers viewed compliance as coercive. This perspective made implementation more difficult, and caused many in the agricultural community to view NRCS as a regulatory agency. This resulted in several congressional oversight hearings to explore implementation of compliance following enactment.

NRCS continues to conduct compliance status reviews on farm and ranch lands that have received USDA benefits and which are subject to the conservation compliance provisions (highly erodible land, wetland compliance, or both). A compliance status review is an inspection of a cropland tract to determine whether the USDA farm program beneficiary is in compliance with the conservation compliance provisions (Table 2). The review process requires an NRCS employee to make an on-site determination when a violation is suspected, and ensures that only qualified NRCS employees report violations. Ultimately, penalties for noncompliance are determined by FSA. Penalties may range from a good faith exemption that allows producers up to one year to correct the violation, to a determination that the producer is ineligible for any government payment and must pay back current and prior years' benefits.

ISSUES FOR CONGRESS

The 1985 farm bill created the highly erodible land conservation and wetland conservation compliance provisions, which tied various farm program benefits to conservation standards. These provisions have been amended with each subsequent farm bill. As the 113th Congress continues to debate the reauthorization of farm programs, issues related to conservation compliance have been raised.

Crop Insurance Linkage

The 1996 farm bill made several changes to conservation programs (see **Appendix A**). It not only strengthened voluntary incentive conservation programs but also lessened the effect on certain conservation compliance provisions. Most notably, the 1996 farm bill removed crop insurance as a program benefit that could be denied, and added production flexibility contracts—now referred to as direct payments. The debate surrounding this decision centered on the policy goal of encouraging producers to purchase crop insurance while responding to farmer concerns that compliance requirements were too intrusive.

Currently, the major farm program benefits that could be affected by compliance are direct payments, counter-cyclical payments, and payments under conservation programs. High commodity prices in recent years have resulted in few or no counter-cyclical payments. This leaves conservation program participation and direct payments as the remaining major benefits that could motivate producer compliance with conservation requirements. The current budgetary climate has caused direct payments under the farm commodity support programs to come under considerable scrutiny. Both the House- and Senate-passed versions of the 2013 farm bill (H.R. 2642 and S. 954) would eliminate direct payments, in part as a budget saving measure, and to replace them with different support programs.[18] Conservation advocates worry that without direct payments there will be little incentive for producers to meet conservation compliance and wetland conservation requirements.

Table 2. Summary of Conservation Compliance Status Reviews

2007		2008	2009	2010	2011
Total Tracts Reviewed	20,134	22,755	20,474	18,704	22,210
Total Acres Reviewed (approx.)	3.3 million	3 million	3 million	3.3 million	2.75 million
Tracts Out of Compliance	276	333	277	344	530
Highly Erodible Land Violation	177	211	177	167	372
Wetland Conservation Violation	99	122	100	177	158
Percentage Out of Compliance	1.4%	1.5%	1.4%	1.8%	2.4%
Number of States Recording Non-Compliance	33	34	30	28	32
Variances or Exemptions Issued	746	880	726	732	887

Source: USDA, NRCS, complied by CRS.

The solution offered by some is to re-couple conservation compliance with crop insurance premium subsidies. Crop insurance is purchased by a producer growing an insurable crop and a percentage of the premium (averaging about 60% of the total) is paid for by the federal government.[19]

The reaction to tying crop insurance to compliance requirements is mixed. Most in the conservation and environmental community support the requirement, while some producer groups and the crop insurance industry are wary of the linkage. In May 2013, a coalition of conservation, environmental, crop insurance, and producer groups sent a letter to the House and Senate

Agriculture Committees supporting a compromise on the issue of benefits affected by conservation compliance.[20] The group supports re-tying conservation compliance to crop insurance benefits in exchange for no means testing, payment limits, or other premium subsidy reductions. While the signatories represent a diverse group of agricultural constituents,[21] a number of other industry and environmental organizations declined to support the compromise, stating that the deal either went too far in limiting crop insurance or did not go far enough in reforming and reducing government support for crop insurance. Amendments adopted during the House floor debate resulted in some organizations pulling support for the letter, while others continued to advocate for the compliance provision.[22]

According to USDA's Economic Research Service (ERS),[23] if direct payments were reduced or eliminated and crop insurance was once again added to the list of possible USDA program benefits subject to conservation compliance, the incentive for compliance could vary depending on location. In areas with higher crop production risk, such as the Northern Plains, crop insurance could provide a compliance incentive that is equal to or even larger than the current one tied to direct payments. In other areas where direct payments offer more of an incentive but crop insurance is not as widely utilized, such as the Mississippi Delta, there might be less incentive to comply with conservation requirements (**Figure 2**).

Erosion and Conversion Rates

The reduction in soil erosion from highly erodible land conservation continues, but at a slower pace than following enactment of the 1985 farm bill (**Figure 3**). The leveling off of reduced erosion leaves several broad policy questions, including whether an acceptable level of soil erosion on cropland has been achieved; whether additional reductions could be achieved, and if so, at what cost; and how federal farm policy should encourage additional reductions in erosion. Some environmental and conservation groups have asked Congress to tighten compliance requirements as one way of reducing soil erosion. Many agricultural groups, however, prefer additional financial incentives through voluntary conservation programs, such as EQIP.

According to USDA's Natural Resource Inventory, in 2007, 99 million acres (28% of all cropland) was eroding above soil loss tolerance (T) rates (see text box).[24] This compares to 169 million acres (40% of cropland) in 1982. Between 1982 and 2007, farmers reduced total cropland soil erosion by 43%

(**Figure 3**). The bulk of this reduction occurred following the 1985 farm bill and the implementation of CRP and conservation compliance requirements. Reduction in soil erosion may also be attributed to other factors. Estimates indicate that compliance provisions could be responsible for approximately 295 million tons, or 25% of the 1.2 billion ton reduction in cropland soil erosion that occurred between 1982 and 1997 (most recent information available).[25] Another 31%, or 365 million tons reduced could be attributed to land use changes, including CRP enrollment.[26]

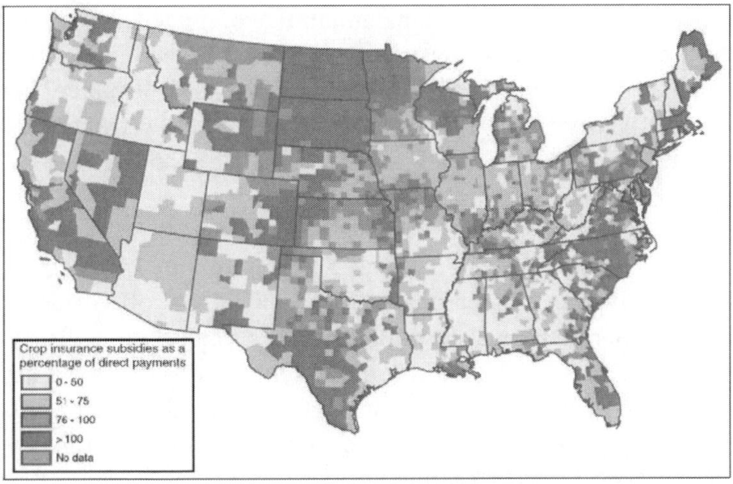

Source: Roger Claassen, The Future of Environmental Compliance Incentives in U.S. Agriculture: The Role of Commodity, Conservation, and Crop Insurance Programs, USDA, ERS, Bulletin No. 94, Washington, DC, March 2012, http://www.ers.usda.gov/Publications/EIB94/EIB94.pdf.

Notes: County-level estimates based on average direct payments and crop insurance subsidies.

Figure 2. County-Level Crop Insurance Subsidies and Direct Payments, 2005-2010.

Funding and program authority for CRP expired on September 30, 2013. House and Senate farm bill proposals (H.R. 2642 and S. 954) would reduce the acreage enrollment in CRP from its current authorized level of 32 million acres to 24 million and 25 million acres, respectively. This could have a potential impact on soil erosion, the magnitude of which is unclear.

In addition to soil erosion reductions following the 1985 farm bill, the number of wetlands converted to cropland was also reduced. Unlike the highly erodible land conservation provision, the impact of the wetland conservation provision is increasingly difficult to measure.

The "T" Factor

Soil erosion occurs for a variety of natural and manmade reasons. An evaluation of different soil types and surrounding conditions (e.g., soil depth, slope, etc.) allows soil scientists to determine what an "acceptable" rate of soil erosion is for a given area. This is commonly referred to as "T" or soil loss tolerance rate. T is the maximum rate of annual soil loss that will permit crop productivity to be sustained economically and indefinitely on a given soil. Erosion is considered to be greater than T if either the water (sheet and rill) erosion or the wind erosion rate exceeds the soil loss tolerance rate. The higher the T value, the more soil erosion can be tolerated.

The use of T is one of the bases for identifying highly erodible land associated with conservation compliance. The erodibility index for a soil is determined by dividing the potential average annual rate of erosion for each soil by its predetermined soil loss tolerance (T) value.[27] T is also used as one of the criteria for planning soil conservation systems required by conservation compliance. Conservationists focus on reducing soil loss to or below T by applying practices, such as terraces, contour strips, grassed waterways, and residue management.

The use of T has been and will likely remain controversial. Some soil scientists have suggested that the current values of T far exceed the actual soil formation rates and therefore are not truly "sustainable" (Craig Cox, Andrew Hug, and Nils Bruzelius, *Losing Ground*, Environmental Working Group, April 2011). Despite these concerns, T remains the only commonly used standard by which soil erosion is measured.

Swampbuster is one of several federal, state, and local policies that discourage the conversion of wetlands to other uses.[28] Other farm bill programs, such as the Wetlands Reserve Program (WRP) and CRP, seek to provide a reverse effect and encourage landowners to restore wetlands. Between 1997 and 2007, USDA estimates that the U.S. experienced a net wetlands gain of about 250,000 acres.[29] Sixty percent of the gross loss (440,000 acres) during that time period is attributed to urban and industrial development and 15% is attributed to agriculture. Both the House- and Senate-passed versions of the farm bill would repeal WRP and incorporate the wetland easement function into a new Agricultural Conservation Easement Program.

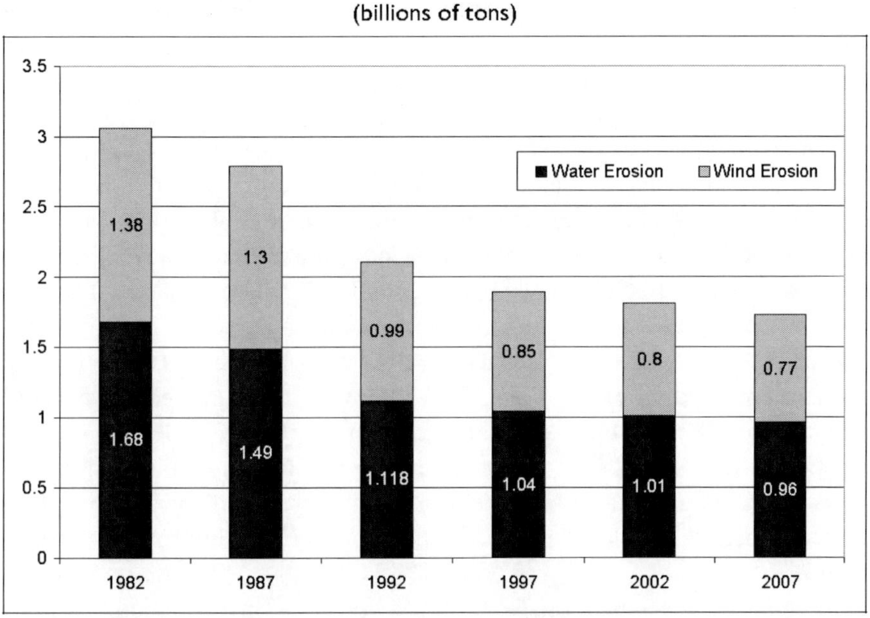

Source: USDA, NRCS, 2007 National Resources Inventory: Soil Erosion on Cropland, April 2010, http://www.nrcs.usda.gov/Internet/FSE_DOCUMENTS/nrcs143_012269.pdf.

Notes: Total includes cultivated and non-cultivated cropland. Water erosion includes sheet and rill erosion.

Figure 3. Soil Erosion on Cropland by Year.

Swampbuster continues to be a controversial provision with some producers. NRCS completes certified wetland determination in response to requests from producers, or in response to whistleblower complaints. With commodity crop prices currently at high levels, producers desire to increase their agricultural production by clearing and/or draining wetlands, and request wetland determinations from the NRCS to ensure compliance with the wetland conservation provision.

This has led to an increased workload for NRCS and could impact the ability of NRCS to provide technical assistance for other farm bill programs.

Oversight

The conservation compliance requirements have undergone several program audits by both the Government Accountability Office (GAO) and USDA's Office of the Inspector General (OIG). The most recent GAO audit was in 2003,[30] which found that many NRCS field offices were not implementing compliance requirements as outlined in the law and issued through agency policy. Reasons for the discrepancy related to a lack of resources, training, and guidance; de-emphasis on compliance relative to other work; and a reluctance to assume an enforcement role. The report noted the lack of NRCS oversight and called into question the accuracy of agency's claims that 98% of tracts reviewed were found to be in compliance. The report also faulted FSA for granting waivers with inadequate documentation. Between 1993 and 2001, FSA waived 4,948 of 8,118 cases (61%) in which farmers were cited with violations. These waivers were granted by local FSA county committees, which generally consist of farmers elected by other farmers in the county. The report stated that NRCS staff and conservation groups believed that the county committees were predisposed to approve farmers' appeals so as not to penalize a neighbor's eligibility for farm program benefits.

In 2008, OIG issued phase I of a two-phase investigation.[31] Phase I evaluated changes to the status review process based on prior audit recommendations made by GAO and OIG. According to the report, NRCS addressed concerns from the previous GAO and OIG investigations by implementing improvements on the sampling methodology and the process by which conservation compliance status review results are summarized, analyzed, and reported. The report found that between 2002 and 2006, the average rate of compliance reported by NRCS was 98%.32 Between 1993 and 2005, a total of $125 million in program benefits was subject to withholding due to compliance violations. Of this total, FSA issued good faith exemptions and restored $103 million (83%) in program benefits. The OIG report concluded that the number of compliance violations reported by NRCS was too low and the number of restored benefits issued by FSA was too high. Phase II is intended to evaluate the effectiveness of the status review process through field inspections and possibly provide an explanation for the high rate of reinstated benefits. To date, no report or status on phase II has been released.

The 2008 farm bill (Section 2002) amended the compliance provisions to include a second level of review for waivers granted by FSA. The conference report cited the changes as "resolv[ing] a long-standing problem and provid[ing] for increased oversight of the violation process."[33] Opinions vary on how well USDA is enforcing the conservation compliance provisions. Environmental organizations advocate for more consistent and rigorous status reviews. Producer organizations advocate for continued flexibility and more additional voluntary programs incentives to support any necessary improvements.

CONCLUSION

As Congress continues to consider the reauthorization of farm policy in the next omnibus farm bill, there is considerable pressure to reduce federal spending. While most farm organizations prefer voluntary financial incentive programs to policies such as conservation compliance, increasing or maintaining funding levels for such financial incentives could be challenging. Some point to the use of agricultural conservation compliance provisions as a way to discourage the degradation of private lands without increasing federal spending. This approach, however, has historically met with controversy, which seems likely to continue.

APPENDIX A. A BRIEF LEGISLATIVE HISTORY OF CONSERVATION COMPLIANCE

Prior to the 1985 farm bill, approximately two dozen soil and water conservation programs existed. These programs reflected a pattern that was established in the 1930s—voluntary cooperation from land users and incentive-based programs—and changed little in 50 years. The expansion of agricultural production in the 1970s to respond to growing world demand for farm products was accompanied by an increase in soil erosion.[34] Much of this erosion was attributed to producers expanding their acreage into "marginal" land—land that easily erodes and is often less productive. Intense production practices were supported by many of the federal farm policies in place at the time.

In 1977, Congress enacted the Soil and Water Resources Conservation Act (P.L. 95-192, referred to as the RCA). The RCA required USDA to appraise the nation's natural resources on nonfederal land and provide

Congress with an annual evaluation report. Many of the soil and water resource issues were highlighted in the 1980 RCA report and drew attention to the high societal cost of soil erosion and wetland conservation that resulted from intense production.[35] As part of the National Program for Soil and Water Conservation, USDA presented the alternative of "cross-compliance," in which farmers who receive USDA benefits would be required to meet minimum conservation standards.[36]

In the early 1980s, large-scale commodity surpluses of certain agricultural products developed from weak global demand and advances in agricultural productivity. In response, during the 1985 farm bill debate, Congress sought new farm policies to increase export markets and reduce domestic production, thereby reducing surpluses. The result was what some classified as a radical departure from the traditional conservation approach.

1985 Farm Bill

The Food Security Act of 1985 (P.L. 99-198, 1985 farm bill) included a number of significant conservation provisions designed to reduce production and conserve soil and water resources. The Conservation Reserve Program (CRP), as authorized in the 1985 farm bill, was allowed to remove up to 45 million acres of land from production under multi-year rental agreements. The financial incentives of CRP far exceeded those of most early conservation programs, and CRP remains the largest conservation program (in terms of funding) to date.[37] The other conservation provisions were highly erodible land conservation (sodbuster) and wetland conservation (swampbuster). Despite the historic significance of these provisions there was surprisingly little debate recorded at the time.

Sodbuster

The highly erodible land conservation provision, as enacted in the 1985 farm bill, introduced the requirement that in exchange for certain federal farm benefits a producer must implement a minimum level of conservation. The provision applies the loss of benefits to land classified as highly erodible that was not in cultivation between 1980 and 1985 (i.e., newly broken land, referred to as sodbuster) and any highly erodible land in production after 1990, regardless of when the land was put into production. Land meeting this classification could be considered eligible for USDA program benefits if the land user agreed to cultivate the land using an approved conservation plan.

There were two main exceptions. First, the farmer had until January 1, 1990, or two years after the completion of a soil survey—whichever was later—to be actively applying an approved conservation plan. Second, if a farmer was actively applying an approved conservation plan, then they had until January 1, 1995, to be full in compliance with the plan. The program benefits that could be lost included:

- price supports and related payments,
- farm storage facility loans,
- crop insurance,
- disaster payments,
- any farm loans that will contribute to excessive erosion of highly erodible land, and
- storage payments made to producers for crops acquired by the Commodity Credit Corporation (CCC).

Swampbuster

The "swampbuster" or wetland conservation provision extends the sodbuster requirement to wetland areas. Producers who plant a program crop on a converted wetland would be ineligible for certain USDA program benefits. The most controversial debate over the swampbuster provision was on the definition of an affected wetland areas. This resulted in many wetland areas being exempt, including:

- wetlands converted before enactment (December 23, 1985),
- artificially created lakes, ponds, or wetlands,
- wetlands created by irrigation delivery systems,
- wetlands on which agricultural production is naturally possible, or
- wetlands converted if the effect of such action is minimal.

Changes Since the 1985 Farm Bill

Since the enactment of the 1985 farm bill, each succeeding farm bill has amended the compliance provisions (both highly erodible land and wetland conservation).

1990 Farm Bill

The compliance provisions were amended in several ways in the Food, Agriculture, Conservation, and Trade Act of 1990 (P.L. 101-624, 1990 farm bill). Conservation provisions were expanded to include wetlands converted after enactment (November 28, 1990), where agricultural commodity production was made possible. This meant that crop production did not actually have to occur in order to be found out of compliance, only that production was made possible through activities such as draining, dredging, filling, or leveling the wetland. The 1990 farm bill added six more federal farm programs to the list of benefits that could be lost for non-compliance, including many of the conservation programs. A graduated penalty was added so that under some circumstances, producers could be subject to a loss in benefits of between \$500 and \$5000. This graduated penalty may be applied only once every five years. The revisions protect tenant farmers who may be ruled out of compliance because of the actions of the landowner or previous tenants. Compliance exemptions were also expanded to include highly erodible land set aside, or taken out of production, under the commodity support programs.

1996 Farm Bill

Beginning in 1994, conservation policy discussions in Congress focused on identifying ways to make the compliance programs less intrusive on farmer activities. As a result, conservation compliance provisions were significantly amended in the Federal Agricultural Improvement and Reform Act of 1996 (P.L. 104-127, referred to as the 1996 farm bill). Many of the conservation compliance changes enacted in the 1996 farm bill were meant to provide producer flexibility and reduce the impact on farm operations. Some of the major amendments to highly erodible land conservation compliance in the 1996 farm bill include:

- removing crop insurance from the list of benefits that could be lost if the farmer is found out of compliance;
- adding production flexibility contracts[38] to the list of benefits that could be lost if found out of compliance;
- highly erodible land exiting CRP would not be held to a higher compliance standard than nearby cropland;
- providing violators with up to one year to meet compliance requirements;
- developing procedures to expedite variances for weather, pest, or disease problems;
- requiring an erosion measurement before the conservation system is implemented;
- allowing third parties to measure residue and require that residue measurements take into account the top two inches of soil;
- allowing producers to modify plans as long as the same level of treatment is maintained;
- allowing local county committees to permit relief if a conservation system causes a producer undue economic hardship; and
- establishing a wind erosion estimation pilot study to review and modify as necessary wind erosion factors used to administer conservation compliance.

Several changes were made in the 1996 farm bill to the wetland conservation provisions as well. Similar to the provisions for highly erodible land, wetland conservation provisions were meant to provide greater program flexibility. Major changes included:

- exempting swampbuster penalties when wetland values and functions are voluntarily restored following a specified procedure;
- providing that prior converted wetlands will not be considered "abandoned" as long as the land is only used for agriculture;
- giving the Secretary of Agriculture discretion to determine which program benefits violators are ineligible for and to provide good-faith exemptions;
- establishing a pilot mitigation banking program (using the CRP);
- repealing required consultation with the U.S. Fish and Wildlife Service; and
- expanding the definition of agricultural lands used in a 1994 interagency Memorandum of Agreement.

While the 1996 farm bill reduced the impact of the compliance requirements it also expanded the voluntary incentive-based programs for agricultural conservation. For the first time the majority of conservation funding was authorized as mandatory funding.[39] Total funding levels for conservation were increased. The conservation agenda was also broadened by adding wildlife considerations and evaluating nonpoint source pollution from agricultural sources.

2002 Farm Bill

The Food Security and Rural Investment Act of 2002 (P.L. 107-171, 2002 farm bill) continued and expanded many of the conservation priorities in the 1996 farm bill, especially those related to voluntary incentive programs and increased funding. Few changes were made to the conservation compliance provisions. The primary change was the requirement that USDA not delegate authority to other parties to make highly erodible land determinations. Also, any person who had highly erodible land enrolled in the CRP was given two years after a contract expires to be in full compliance.

2008 Farm Bill

The Food, Conservation and Energy Act of 2008 (P.L. 110-246, referred to as the 2008 farm bill) again made few changes to the conservation compliance provisions. The primary change was the addition of a second level of review by the state or district FSA director, with technical concurrence from the state or area NRCS conservationist if USDA determines that this exception should apply.

Appendix B. FSA and NRCS Responsibilities

Table B-1. FSA and NRCS Responsibilities Administering Conservation Compliance on Highly Erodible Land

FSA Responsibilities[a]	
• Establish field/tract boundaries, field numbers, and acreage	• Consult with NRCS about the adequacy of conservation systems as needed

FSA Responsibilities[a]	
• Determine whether a tenant is required to produce an agricultural commodity on highly erodible land under the terms and conditions of an agreement between the landlord and the tenant or sharecropper	• Determine whether a producer violated the conservation compliance provisions (both highly erodible land conservation and wetland conservation)
• Determine whether an individual, joint venture, or entity is a producer on a highly erodible field or converted wetland	• Notify new owners and operators of a tract of previous determinations and the status of conservation system on the tract
• Determine whether the land meets the sodbuster provisions (i.e., was converted from native vegetation, such as grassland, rangeland, or woodland, to agricultural production after December 23, 1985)	• Determine whether proceeds of a farm program loan made, insured, or guaranteed by FSA-Farm Credit will be used for a purpose that will contribute to excessive erosion on highly erodible land or to the conversion of a wetland to produce an agricultural commodity
• Determine if the conversion of a wetland was caused by a third party	• Determine whether persons qualify for a good faith exemption
• Provide general supervision for day-to-day conservation compliance operations	• Determine on request whether application of a conservation system causes a person undue economic hardship
• Refer cases requiring a technical determination to NRCS	• Provide producers with appeal rights and mediation
• Obtain producer's certification of intentions to comply with conservation compliance requirements	• Consult with NRCS about determinations of third-party conversion
• Determine the accuracy of a producers certification according to the spot-check procedures	• Make determinations of ineligibility for certain program benefits, as violations are discovered
NRCS Responsibilities[b]	
• Provide technical assistance for conservation planning when requested, and applying conservation systems to the land upon request	• Complete compliance reviews that are (1) regularly scheduled, (2) in response to an FSA request, and (3) in response to a whistleblower complaint

Table B-1. (Continued)

NRCS Responsibilities[b]	
• Make determinations for highly erodible soil map units and the predominance of highly erodible land in a field	• Provide assistance for conservation system revisions for USDA participant reinstatement
• Determine whether land meets wetland criteria and whether a wetland exemption applies (see those listed above)	• Provide FSA with information for making tenant exemption determinations and provide conservation planning assistance to the tenant
• Determine qualifications for temporary variances from the requirements of a conservation system	• Provide FSA with information for making good faith exemptions
• Identify NRCS error or misinformation	• Apply a conservation system that meets the soil reduction and/or improvement criteria.

a. As outlined in USDA Farm Service Agency, *Highly Erodible Land Conservation and Wetland Conservation Provisions*, FSA Handbook 6-CP (revision3), Washington, DC, http://www.fsa.usda.gov/Internet/FSA_File/6-cp.pdf.

b. As outlined in USDA Natural Resources Conservation Service, *National Food Security Act Manual*, *Fifth Edition,* M_180_NFSM_510, November 2010.

End Notes

[1] C RP is not discussed in depth in this report. For additional information and issues related to CRP reauthotization, see CRS Report R42093, *Agricultural Conservation and the Next Farm Bill.*

[2] Highly erodible land conservation and wetland conservation are collectively referred to as conservation compliance in this report.

[3] A list of conference designees may be found here: http://agriculture.house.gov/press-release/first-public-meeting- 2013-farm-bill-conference-committee-announced.

[4] For additional information on the federal crop insurance program, see CRS Report R40532, *Federal Crop Insurance: Background.*

[5] H.Amdt. 188.

[6] In 2012, an average of 63% of the total crop insurance premium was paid for by the federal government, and the remainder by the participating farmer. The Senate-passed sodsaver provision would reduce a producer's crop insurance premium subsidy by 50 percentage points if found out of compliance. For example, a 50 percentage point reduction would lower a premium subsidy rate of 63% to 13%.

[7] The House-passed bill establishes the T-yield factor at no more than 70% of the 10-year average county yield for general cropland (§11009) and 65% for native sod (§11013).

[8] The Senate-passed bill increases the T-yield factor to no more than 65% of the 10-year average county yield for both general cropland (§11007) and native sod (§11035).

[9] Under current law, if one or more of the crop years used to establish the producer's actual production history is less than 60% of the T-yield, then it is either excluded or replaced with a yield equal to 60% of the T-yield (7 U.S.C. 1508(g)(4)(B)).

[10] 16 U.S.C. 3822(f)(2).

[11] §2609 of H.R. 2642.

[12] §2508 of S. 954.

[13] USDA, Soil Conservation Service, *Land Capability Classifications System*, Agricultural Handbook 210, Washington, DC, 1961, ftp://ftp-fc.sc.egov.usda.gov/NSSC/LCC/handbook_210.pdf.

[14] H.Rept. 99-271, p. 84.

[15] Ibid., p. 88.

[16] In addition to those listed, a producer who participated in a USDA program that set aside land for the purpose of reducing production of an agricultural commodity, may also not be considered ineligible. Many of these "set-aside" programs are no longer utilized.

[17] For more information on crop insurance and NAP, see CRS Report R40532, *Federal Crop Insurance: Background* and CRS Report RS21212, *Agricultural Disaster Assistance*.

[18] For more information, see CRS Report R42759, *Farm Safety Net Provisions in a 2013 Farm Bill: S. 954 and H.R. 2642.*

[19] The government-paid portion of crop insurance premiums can range between 38% to 80% of the total premium. A producer's premium for a policy increases as the levels of insurable yield and price coverage rise, and the premium on buy-up coverage is subsidized by the government depending on the coverage level. The subsidy rate declines as the coverage level rises, but the total premium subsidy in dollars increases because the policies are more expensive. In total, the government cost for crop insurance programs was $14.1 billion in FY2012. Insurance policies are sold and completely serviced through 15 approved private insurance companies; however, the insurance companies' losses are reinsured by USDA, and their administrative and operating costs are reimbursed by the federal government. For additional information, see CRS Report R40532, *Federal Crop Insurance: Background*.

[20] A copy of the letter may be found here: http://www.nacdnet.org/news/newsroom/2013/groups-call-for-conservationcompliance- compromise.

[21] Signatories of the letters include American Association of Crop Insurers, American Farm Bureau Federation, American Soybean Association, Ducks Unlimited, Environmental Defense Fund, National Association of Conservation Districts, National Corn Growers Association, National Cotton Council, National Farmers Union, Pheasants Forever, National Wildlife Federation, The Nature Conservancy, and the World Wildlife Fund.

[22] Amena H. Saiyid, "Farm Bureau Will Not Back Agreement to Link Crop Insurance to Conservation," *Bloomberg BNA Daily Environment Report*, October 18, 2013, pp. 202 DEN A-15 and Christopher Doering, "Environmental groups urge Congress to tie crop insurance to conservation," *DesMoines Register*, October 30, 2013, pp. http://blogs.desmoinesregister.com/dmr/index.php/2013/10/30/environmental-groups-urge-congress-to-tie-cropinsurance- to-conservation/article.

[23] Roger Claassen, The Future of Environmental Compliance Incentives in U.S. Agriculture: The Role of Commodity, Conservation, and Crop Insurance Programs, USDA, ERS, Bulletin No. 94, Washington, DC, March 2012, http://www.ers.usda.gov/Publications/ EIB94/EIB94.pdf.

[24] USDA, NRCS, *2007 National Resources Inventory: Soil Erosion on Cropland*, April 2010, http://www.nrcs.usda.gov/Internet/FSE_DOCUMENTS/nrcs143_012269.pdf.

[25] Roger Claassen, "Have Conservation Compliance Incentives Reduced Soil Erosion?" USDA, ERS, *Amber Waves*, June 2004, http://www.ers.usda.gov/AmberWaves/June04/Features/HaveConservation.htm.

[26] Ibid.

[27] 7 C.F.R. §12.21(a).

[28] The other major federal policy is Section 404 of the Clean Water Act. For additional information, see CRS Report RL33483, *Wetlands: An Overview of Issues*.

[29] USDA, *RCA Appraisal: Soil and Water Resources Conservation Act*, Washington, DC, July 2011, http://www.nrcs.usda.gov/Internet/FSE_DOCUMENTS/stelprdb1044939.pdf.

[30] U.S. GAO, *Agricultural Conservation: USDA needs to better ensure protection of highly erodible cropland and wetlands*, GAO-03-418, April 2003, http://www.gao.gov/assets/240/ 237878.pdf.

[31] USDA, Office of the Inspector General, *Audit Report: Natural Resources Conservation Service Status Review Process*, Report No. 50601-13-KC, Great Plains Region, June 2008.

[32] Specifically on average, 58% were found to be in compliance, 37% required no conservation plan because no highly erodible land was present or if wetlands were present there was no violation found, 3% were found to be out of compliance but granted variances (e.g., weather, pest, disease exemptions), and 2% were found to be out of compliance.

[33] H.Rept. 110-627.

[34] J. Douglas Helms, *Leveraging Farm Policy for Conservation: Passage of the 1985 Farm Bill*, USDA, Natural Resources Conservation Service, Historical Insights Number 6, June 2006, http://www.nrcs.usda.gov/Internet/ FSE_DOCUMENTS/stelprdb1044129.pdf.

[35] U.S. Department of Agriculture, *Summary of Appraisal, Parts I and II, and Program Report*, GPO 1980 633- 769/460, 1980.

[36] U.S. Department of Agriculture, *A National Program for Soil and Water Conservation*, 1982 Final Program Report and Environmental Impact Statement, GPO 1982-0-522-010/3711, September 1982.

[37] CRP is currently authorized to enroll up to 32 million acres and annually spends an average of over $2 billion in mandatory funding. The purpose of CRP has long been debated. In its early years, some believed the program's sole purpose was for production control. Others saw CRP as a soil erosion control program. Today, many view it as a wildlife habitat program. The program's objectives and purpose are not debated in this report. For additional information and issues related to CRP reauthotization, see CRS Report R42093, *Agricultural Conservation and the Next Farm Bill*.

[38] Producer flexibility contracts are now referred to as direct payments.

[39] Mandatory funding is made available by multiyear authorizing legislation and does not require annual appropriations or subsequent action by Congress.

INDEX

D

E

F

G

H

I

L

M

N

O